# KIDS EXPLORE AMERICA'S JAPANESE AMERICAN HERITAGE

## 2nd Edition

*Westridge Young Writers Workshop*

John Muir Publications
Santa Fe, New Mexico

*When you read this book you will learn*
*All kinds of people make the world turn.*
*Each is different in his or her own way,*
*We want you to know that that's OK.*
*These heroes have taught us things we didn't know,*
*Now along with us you can grow.*

John Muir Publications, P.O. Box 613, Santa Fe, NM 87504
Copyright © 1996, 1994 by Jefferson County School District N. R-1
Cover © 1994 by John Muir Publications

Printed in the United States of America
Second edition. First printing September 1996

Library of Congress Cataloging-in-Publication Data
Kids explore America's Japanese American heritage / Westridge Young
   Writers Workshop. — 2nd ed.
   p.          cm.
   Summary: Presents writings by students in grades three to seven on topics of Japanese
American culture, including sports, cooking, history, and art.
   Includes index.
   ISBN 1-56261-273-5 (pbk.)
   1. Japanese Americans—Juvenile literature. 2. Children's writings, American. [1. Japanese
Americans. 2. Children's writings]          I. Westridge Young Writers Workshop.
E184.J3K454 1996
973'.04956—dc20

                                                                                        96-37
                                                                                        CIP
                                                                                        AC

**Editors** Rob Crisell, Peggy Schaefer, Heidi Utz
**Production** Nikki Rooker, Marie Vigil
**Graphics Manager** Sarah Horowitz
**Design** Susan Surprise
**Cover Art** Tony D'Agostino
**Map** on page 16 by Jim and Holly Wood
**Typesetting** Jaye Oliver
**Printer** Publishers Press

Distributed to the book trade by
Publishers Group West
Emeryville, California

# CONTENTS

# ACKNOWLEDGMENTS

We, the 94 student authors, are especially appreciative of the people of Japanese American heritage who shared their time and talent with us. A book like this takes the help of many people. Lots of individuals and groups contributed in preparing the outline, doing research, presenting programs, providing resources, teaching dancing, assisting in the art room, helping with cooking, picking up supplies, or serving in other ways. The following are some of the people who made a significant contribution:

Carrie Ann Aoki
Yuri Ariki
Art Arita
Itsu Arita
Tom Beston
Monica Cetuk
Gaylene Endo
Marcia Everson
Jeanne Fagen
Mary Ferguson
Carol Fujioka
Robin Furuta
Eva Hafer
Hideo Hamamura
Yoshi Hamamura

Rev. George Hanabusa
Debbie Harmon
Dr. Lane Hirabayashi
Irene Hirano
Frank Hiraoka
Lorraine Hisamoto
Roy Inouye
Yoshiko Inouye
Craig Iriye
Virgie Ito
Jane Kano
Debbie Kawakami
Kathryn Kawakami
Alison Kochiyama
Tay Kondo
Rev. Eijun Kujo
Kats Kunitsugu
Sadaharu Kurobane
Kim Manning
D'ann Masaki
Archie Miyatake
Theresa Montoya
Roy Nagai
Kathy Namura
Catherine Nelson
Brian Niiya
Nobuko Ninomiya
Mary Nishiyama
Sandy Noguchi
Rev. Kanya Okamoto

Rose Roy
Carol Saito
Ellen Sakamoto
Wes Sakamoto
Janet Sasa
Cindie Shibata
Ruth Shinto
Pat Stromberg
Mickey Takeshita
Jimmy Tokeshi
Candy Tsutsui
Lillian Uba
Reiko Urano
Sue Uyeda
Aaron Velarde
Arlene Wada
Suzie Weaver
Christine Wanifuchi
Sandy Yamakishi
Ruth Yamauchi
Lulu Yip
Kent Yoritomo

Organizations, churches, temples, and businesses that assisted with presentations, merchandise, or money include the following:

Denver Buddhist Temple
Denver Buddhist Temple Judo Dojo
Denver Central Optimists
Denver Japanese Karate Center and Team
Denver Wholesale Florist
FirstBank of South Jeffco
Fort Lupton Japanese American Citizens League
Japanese American Curriculum Project
Japanese American National Museum
Jr. Denver Taiko Group
Los Angeles Japanese American Citizens League
Military Intelligence Veterans Club
Mums the Word
Pacific Mercantile
*Rafu Shimpo* newspaper
Simpson United Methodist Church
Sun newspaper
Toyo Miyatake Studios
*Tozai Times*
U.S. West Foundation

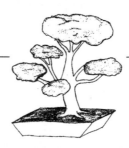

# TEACHERS' PREFACE

*We accept the challenge of building a brighter
future. We will not ignore the problems caused by
racism in America. We pledge to continue to work
for respect for all Americans.*

The fourth book in the Kids Explore series, *Kids Explore America's Japanese American Heritage*, is a product of the Westridge Young Writers Workshop. The workshop was a ten-day writing project held at Westridge Elementary School in Jefferson County, a western suburb of Denver, Colorado.

Ninety-four students, ages eight to 14, participated in researching, writing, organizing, editing, and illustrating the information that became this book. In addition, 35 teachers and 19 high-school mentors contributed their expertise, helping the authors learn about history, food, celebrations, the arts, folk tales, and literature, as well as about real people and heroes. The majority of the students and teachers who participated in this project are Japanese American.

Each person in the workshop took part in all the activities, from making artwork, cooking recipes, and watching demonstrations, to learning Japanese words, singing songs, and writing for a section of the book. By participating in all of the activities, the authors developed an appreciation for Japanese American culture as a whole, then shared their knowledge of one aspect of it. The older students wrote the history section. They were able to understand the past and then write about it in a way that young readers can understand. The younger students kept the older authors on track, making sure they used interesting, accessible language.

While the authors worked on enhancing their research and writing skills, the teachers earned graduate college credit through a course entitled "Integrating Japanese American Studies into the School Curriculum."

As we learned more about Japanese American heritage, we also explored ways to integrate cultures into school curricula.

One of these ways is through language. This book introduces a number of Japanese words and names, and provides a pronunciation key for all of them. There are five basic vowel sounds in Japanese:

A sounds like "ah," as in "father"
E sounds like "eh," as in "get"
I sounds like "ee," as in "machine"
O sounds like "oh," as in "hope"
U sounds like "oo," as in "flu"

Accented syllables are not used in the Japanese language. Therefore, we do not show a stressed syllable. Syllables are divided after the vowels, with the exception of those ending in "n" or "m." These are the only consonants that can end a syllable (for example, *sen-sei*). All other consonants begin a syllable. Where double consonants occur, syllables are divided between the two, as in Is-sei.

During this writing project, we became more aware of the cultural diversity of the United States. In addition, we learned that although people across our country have many different cultural backgrounds, they are all proud to be Americans. In fact, many Japanese Americans who have vacationed in Japan discovered that they are very American indeed, and not Japanese. The diversity of heritage that makes up our country brings a richness to it that blends the past with the present.

As teachers, we have developed a better understanding of diversity, which we can pass on to our students. We have also become more sensitive to and appreciative of Japanese American culture and traditions. It is our hope that this book will contribute to a greater understanding of the many rich cultures in our nation.

# HISTORY

*Ethnic history should not be ignored,*
*Read while you learn and pride will be restored.*
*Remember this chapter about people, struggles, and success,*
*So you will learn to do your very best.*

This section is about Japanese American history—and lots of it! We believe we have written this in a way you can understand. We've included information that gets left out of most children's history books. Japanese Americans are now on a successful path, but to get to this point, they have had to face and overcome prejudice and discrimination.

## EARLY JAPANESE IMMIGRATION TO AMERICA

In 1841 in Japan, a young man named Manjiro Nakahama went fishing with four friends. A storm swept their boat to a small island in the Pacific. Months later, they were rescued by an American sea captain named William Whitfield, who took them to Hawaii. There they waited for a chance to go back to Japan.

When their chance finally came, Mr. Nakahama decided to go to New England with Captain Whitfield. He learned English and attended school in Massachusetts. About ten years later, Mr. Nakahama went back to Japan to visit his family. He also helped the Japanese government understand the Americans.

Around 1851, another Japanese boat was stranded at sea. The crew floated for 50 days on the ocean before they were picked up by an American ship and taken to San Francisco. These Japanese sailors were not allowed to go ashore. They had to stay on board the ship for a long time while plans were made to return them to Japan. It was hard to get the sailors home, because Japanese law then said that foreign ships could not go to Japan. Finally, arrangements were made for the men to be sent home.

One of these sailors was named Hikozo Hamada. Mr. Hamada was encouraged by an American man to stay in the United States, learn English, and help the governments of Japan and the United States become friendlier. Mr. Hamada was even taken to meet President Lincoln. After some

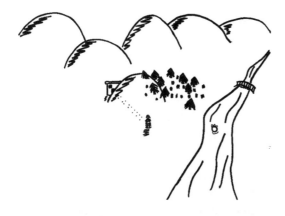

time in the U.S., he changed his name to Joseph Heco, because it sounded pleasant and more American to him. Mr. Heco became the first person born in Japan to become an American citizen.

Before the mid-1800s, Japanese law prohibited people from other countries from going to Japan, and Japanese people could not leave their country. Some Japanese didn't want outsiders' ideas in their country, so Mr. Nakahama and Mr. Heco were very unusual. This law was challenged by an American naval officer, Matthew C. Perry, who wanted Japanese ports open to foreign trade. In 1853, Admiral Perry led some warships into Edo Bay, now known as Tokyo Bay. He demanded that Japan allow foreigners into the country. The Japanese government finally agreed to let people visit Japan. The following year, the United States and Japan signed a formal treaty, freeing up trade between the two countries.

In 1868, the first group of Japanese left for the United States. These people established the Wakamatsu Colony at Gold Hill in northern California. Although their colony failed, many other Japanese pioneers would follow in about a decade.

## IMMIGRATION IN THE LATE 1800s

After Japan agreed to trade with the United States in the late 1800s, many Japanese men decided to cross the Pacific Ocean for education, work, and adventure. Many of the earliest travelers were students sent by the Japanese government to get an education in the West. These students were supposed to return to Japan to help the Japanese understand American ways. Others just wanted a better education in the United States.

There were other reasons Japanese men left Japan. In Japan, a family's oldest son inherited all the family property. Many men who were not firstborn moved to America to get land of their own. Also, taxes in Japan were so high that some people had to leave or sell their land. A few left because they had broken the law and didn't want to get caught or punished. Another reason to leave was that all men between the ages of 20 and 32 had to join the army. Stories in the newspapers told about the success of Japanese immigrants in the United States. Others dreamed that they could find success, too.

At first, most of the Japanese who moved to America planned to make some money, then go back to Japan to buy land, build a house, and have a family. But it was hard for them to save money. Because land

*A group of Japanese Americans*

Many Japanese men worked on farms as laborers. They were paid by the hour or by the day. They worked in fields on the Pacific Coast, mainly in California, and also in the Rocky Mountain states.

If farm laborers could save enough money, they could become sharecroppers. A sharecropper works on someone else's field and gets part of the money from the crops, not just an hourly wage. After saving even more money, a Japanese person could then rent land from an American. This way he could grow his own crops and keep all the money, not just a part. Once he saved enough money, he could buy his own farm.

Japanese immigrants were successful at farming, because many learned how to take land no one wanted and turn it into usable fields for crops. Every member of the Japanese family worked hard to make the land more productive. They drained swamplands, leveled hillsides, and cleared away forest and brush. Their farming skills, love for the land, and hard work made them successful farmers.

prices in Japan kept rising and immigrants had low-paying jobs in America, many people never saved up enough money to go back to Japan. Instead, they stayed in the United States.

Labor contractors (people who hired others to work in the United States) tried to convince the Japanese to come to America by offering them passage, food, and clothing. They were told that jobs would be waiting for them once they got to America, but these jobs ended up being extremely difficult ones that no one else would do. The Japanese who came to the United States had to have strength, hope, and the courage to leave their own land and journey into the unknown.

Most of the early immigrants went to the West Coast of the United States—California, Oregon, Washington, and Alaska and Hawaii (which later became states). There, labor contractors assigned them different jobs. The Japanese weren't paid very much, but they worked hard just the same.

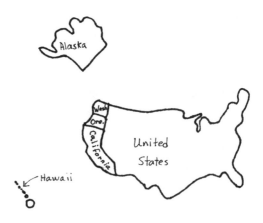

Some white wholesalers were prejudiced against the Japanese and refused to buy from Japanese American farmers. (A wholesaler is a person who buys fruits and vegetables from farmers and then sells them to the stores.) For this reason, many Japanese immigrants opened their own businesses and sold their fruits and vegetables themselves. They sold their produce to other Japanese or to neighbors. By 1940, half the produce on the West Coast was sold by Japanese wholesalers.

Another way the Japanese made a living was by fishing. Since Japan is an island nation, many Japanese immigrants knew how to fish when they came to America. In 1901, a dozen Japanese fishermen arrived at Terminal Island near Los Angeles, California. These fishermen caught fish and abalone in the ocean between Central America and Hawaii. By 1910, Terminal Island had three canneries that employed 3,000 people. Nearly 2,000 of these workers were Japanese. Other Japanese fishermen continued to fish off the coasts of California, Oregon, Washington, and Alaska.

Many Japanese immigrants found jobs that didn't require a lot of English. Some men mined for gold and silver in Utah or for coal in Colorado. They also worked in lumber mills and logging camps in Oregon. Strong Japanese men helped build the railroad tracks in the mountain states like Colorado and Idaho and throughout the West.

Most Japanese immigrants lived on farms, but some lived in the cities. They worked

in houses as cooks, servants, and gardeners. Many people hired Japanese because they were thought to be quiet, honest, and hardworking.

Many other white people didn't like the Japanese and kept away from them. The Japanese looked foreign, talked differently, and ate different foods. These Americans felt that they were better than the Japanese. They didn't trust people from other countries in general.

Most storeowners didn't want the Japanese in their stores, so the Japanese had to open their own businesses to serve their own community. They started restaurants where they cooked Japanese foods. They opened hotels, grocery stores, laundries, and barber shops. They built thriving business centers for their communities.

## JAPANESE WOMEN COME TO AMERICA

There were many Japanese women who arrived in America at the same time as

Carolyn Takeshita

*Picture bride's husband*

Carolyn Takeshita

*Picture bride from Japan*

Japanese men. They came as nurses, students, and laborers. Other women, though, had a different situation.

Imagine you are a young woman, and your father has given you a picture of a man in his 20s. You don't recognize him. Who is he? You finally figure out that it is a picture of a man who wants to marry you!

Today, most people get married because they love each other. But many years ago, marriages were arranged by the parents of the young couple. That's how it was for some early Japanese immigrants. At the beginning of this century, American laws didn't allow non-white people to marry white people. At this time, there were very few Japanese women living in America. The Japanese men who immi-grated to the United States had to come up with a plan to find wives. Between 1900 and 1920, pictures were exchanged and marriages were arranged between families in Japan. The women from these marriages were often called "picture brides."

Sometimes older Japanese men in America would send pictures of themselves at a younger age—or even pictures of a different person! They knew that a young woman would probably want to marry someone her own age. Some of these older men had been saving up money for 20 years to bring their brides to America. Imagine how it would feel to be alone for that long, especially when you are from a culture that values the family as much as the Japanese culture does.

After exchanging pictures, the man would pay for the woman to come to the United States. Before she left Japan, the woman would get married in a traditional Japanese wedding ceremony without the groom. Sometimes the woman would have to live with the husband's family after the wedding until she left for America. The bride and groom often got married again in America.

You might wonder why a woman would choose to be a picture bride. She might have had hopes of becoming rich, or she might have been curious about the distant country called America. Some older women were afraid of never getting married or having children. Most women were not able to support themselves. Other women married because it was their parents' wish. In Japan, especially in those days, you always did what your parents told you to do, no matter how old you were.

The journey to America in the crowded quarters of slow-moving steamships was difficult. Many of the travelers suffered from seasickness and boredom. When the women saw their husbands for the first time, some of them broke down and cried tears of joy or sadness. Some of the brides had dreamed about a rich, handsome man, only to find out that their grooms were much older and not rich at all.

The women had to work in the fields, do housework, grow a garden, and work in shops, all while taking care of a family. Mothers usually had to take their babies with them when they worked in the fields. The babies occasionally died of heat, disease, drowning, or other accidents. If there was an older daughter in the family, she did all of the housework and took care of the children. At times, the husbands were mean, so the friendships women had with one another at work were very important to them.

But if a woman's life was awful in America, she could not return to Japan. Her parents would be ashamed, because people would think their daughter had failed to make a life for herself in America. Many marriages succeeded only because of duty, respect, and honor.

About 70,000 Japanese women came to America (including Hawaii) between 1900 and 1920, but only some of them were picture brides. On February 28, 1920, under pressure from the United States, the Japanese government said that it would not let any more picture brides come to America. This was called the "Ladies Agreement." Many men who did not have wives yet were afraid they would never get married. For the next three or four years, single men had to return to Japan to find their brides themselves.

## GENERATIONS

In order to understand the history of Japanese Americans, it's important to know how each generation is named. The Japanese are the only Asian-Americans who do this. The Japanese word *sei* (pronounced "say") means "generation or an age." *Is* (ees) comes from the word that means "one," so Issei means "first generation." *Ni* (nee) means "two," so Nisei means "second generation." And *san* (sahn) means "three," so Sansei means "third generation." The list below tells you the words for the first through the tenth generations:

*Issei*—first generation
*Nisei*—second generation
*Sansei*—third generation
*Yonsei* (yohn-say)—fourth generation
*Gosei* (goh-say)—fifth generation
*Rokusei* (roh-koo-say)—sixth generation
*Nanasei* (nah-nah-say)—seventh generation
*Hachisei* (hah-chee-say)—eighth generation (also *Hassei,* hah-say)
*Kyusei* (kyoo-say)—ninth generation
*Jissei* (jees-say)—tenth generation

Try to figure out which generation you belong to.

The Issei are people who were born in Japan and came to the United States. Most of them arrived between 1890 and 1924. They were not American citizens by birth, and they weren't allowed to apply for citizenship until after World War II. Most of them were men. Most spoke Japanese, but some learned to speak some English.

The Japanese were among the best-educated immigrants to the United States. Some of them had an eighth-grade education, which was a lot of schooling back then. Others even had college degrees.

Values and family roots were important to the Issei. They knew the importance of education and encouraged their children to study hard. When they were sad, some found strength in their Japanese traditions. They loved one another, and their families were very special to them. They taught their children to respect nature, religion, traditional values, and their elders.

*A produce store in a Japanese American community*

The Issei also valued conformity, which means that they tried not to be different from anyone else in how they looked, talked, or acted. "Saving face" was also very important to them. This means that they avoided doing anything that would cause embarrassment to themselves or to their families. In Japan, farmers, workers, and craftsmen were taught to accept things that happened to them. They were taught to keep quiet and not to complain.

Many Issei helped other newcomers settle into Japanese American communities. They explained American laws and ways, and they helped new people find houses and feel welcome. They also had a saying, *"kodomo no tame ni"* (koh-doh-moh noh tah-meh nee), which means "for the sake of the children." They put up with all the mean things that people said or did to them so that their children might have a good future in America.

The Nisei, or second generation, were the children of the Issei. Most of the Nisei were born between 1900 and 1940. They were born in America, which made them American citizens. This made Nisei different from their Japan-born parents, who would not become naturalized citizens until 1952.

Nisei were raised in two cultures. They often spoke Japanese at home and English at school. They practiced American ways with their friends and Japanese customs with their families. Nisei shared many of the same values as their parents. They went to school in America, with the encouragement of their Issei parents. They also wanted to fit in with American culture. This meant they had to give up some of their Japanese customs and ways.

The *Sansei* (sahn-say) are the third generation. Like their Nisei parents, these Japanese Americans were born in America. They are American citizens, too. Some Issei feel that the Sansei have lost their Japanese traditions, language, and values, because the Sansei dress, talk, act, and think like "Americans." The Sansei generation is known for saying what is on their minds

and for being more willing to stand up for themselves. Most Sansei were born between the mid-1940s and mid-1960s.

The *Yonsei* (yohn-say), or fourth generation, were born into families that had been in the U.S. for 50 years or more. They understand and take part in nearly all American events and customs. Sometimes they practice Japanese culture on special occasions. Most Yonsei have never been to Japan. Most of the authors of this book are Yonsei.

## BUILDING A SENSE OF COMMUNITY

As Japanese immigrants began to settle in America, they formed organizations to help one another. One important group was the *kenjinkai* (kehn-jeen-kye). A ken is similar to a state. People who lived in different kens had their own ways of speaking Japanese, different habits and customs, and even different churches. A kenjinkai helped people from the same ken solve problems and meet other people.

Courtesy of Archie A. Miyatake

*The Koyasan Buddhist Temple*

Contractors would often assign new laborers to work with people from the same ken. Being in a kenjinkai, the laborers could continue to speak their regional dialect of Japanese, eat the food they had eaten in Japan, and carry on trades from their area of Japan.

Religion played a very important part in the lives of many Japanese, and it still does today. Many Japanese don't believe in just one religion, but often combine parts of Buddhism, Shintoism, and Christianity.

In America, many Japanese Americans practiced Buddhism or Christianity. These two religions often worked together in the Japanese American community. They added to the traditional ceremonies for marriage, birth, and death. They helped the Japanese immigrants learn to speak English and adopt American ways. The religions also taught children to be polite with their elders, friends, and strangers. They counseled women about fashion and cooking, and also helped many Japanese Americans find jobs. Some preschoolers and kindergartners took classes in temples and churches.

Within the Japanese American community there were clubs that people belonged to. What purpose did these clubs serve? First, the immigrants wanted to learn about their new home and new culture. Second, young men and women wanted a place to meet and get to know one another. This was good for parents, too, because they often wanted their children to marry "their own kind." Also, Japanese Americans were not allowed to join most white clubs until after World War II.

In the early 1900s, Japanese Americans began to play baseball. The Issei formed their own athletic leagues, because they were not allowed to play in other American leagues. It was their main enjoyment after long hours of hard work. Japanese Americans had baseball teams in many states. As the Nisei became older, they formed baseball teams, too, and there were games played almost every Sunday. Teams had play-offs and even played for the league championship at a state level. Baseball gave

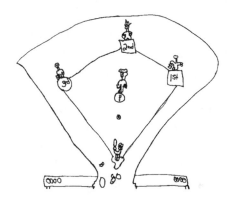

them a chance to make new friends and be part of a Japanese American community.

The Nisei also formed all-Japanese basketball leagues in the late 1930s. They even had Japanese announcers. The Nisei leagues became so popular that they also held statewide and national play-offs.

Other community organizations were often all Japanese American. These included the Boy and Girl Scouts, the YMCAs and YWCAs, the Campfire Girls, gardening associations, bowling leagues, and martial arts. For example, a local YMCA would sponsor a group just for Japanese Americans. These organizations gave Japanese Americans a chance to get together and participate in activities they were excluded from by white people.

## DISCRIMINATION AND EXCLUSION

Throughout American history, laws have been passed against nonwhites. As far back as 1790, Congress passed a law stating that only "free white people" could become citizens of the United States. Then in 1870, Congress changed that law so that people of African descent could become citizens, but other nonwhite immigrants could not.

In 1882, the Chinese Exclusion Act was passed. This stopped Chinese people from legally entering the United States and from becoming American citizens. People who were prejudiced against the Chinese soon became angry when Japanese immigrants came to the United States to do the hard jobs once done by the Chinese.

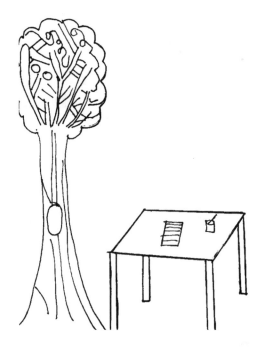

Groups that were prejudiced against the Japanese began forming in the early 1900s. The success of the Issei made these groups angry, because they felt the immigrants were taking their jobs. They robbed and attacked Japanese businesses. Many of these groups influenced lawmakers and government officials. Several politicians gave speeches and tried to pass laws against Japanese immigrants. One man who supported the anti-Japanese groups was James D. Phelan, the mayor of San Francisco. He once said about Japanese immigrants, "They are not the stuff of which American citizens are made."

By 1905, Russia and Japan had just finished a war. Japan had won, and Russia was forced to sign a treaty. Bad feelings against the Japanese started to swell in America. The war had given those who hated the

Japanese an excuse to think that Japan might next try to attack the United States. Lawmakers in California tried to pass laws against the Japanese people each time the legislature met, from 1908 until a few years after World War II.

Another example of prejudice against the Japanese came after the big earthquake of 1906 in San Francisco. The earthquake damaged several schools and gave the San Francisco School Board an excuse to throw nearly 100 Japanese children out of school. They told the kids to go to the "Oriental School" in Chinatown. The school board tried to establish a separate school system for the Japanese. Twenty-five of those children were American citizens of Japanese descent.

The Japanese Association protested because Chinatown was far from many Japanese immigrants' homes. The students and their families were insulted by the school board's action because they valued education and didn't want to be treated differently. Even the Japanese government protested. Even President Theodore Roosevelt described the school board's action as a "wicked absurdity." In late 1907, the president convinced the school board

that they should let the Japanese students back into the regular public school system.

In 1908, President Roosevelt signed the "Gentlemen's Agreement" with Japan, which said that if the Japanese would stop sending workers from Japan, the United States would treat the Japanese in America more fairly. Farm labor groups in California didn't want any more workers from Japan because they felt the Japanese were taking their jobs.

At this time, women and children could still come to America, because the Gentlemen's Agreement allowed Japanese to join family members in the United States. But labor groups soon claimed that Japanese women were taking too many of the jobs and having too many children. Many people didn't like this. They knew that children born in the United States were American citizens, entitled to many of the same rights as other Americans. On March 1, 1920, under a lot of pressure from the United States, the Japanese government stopped giving passports to women, too.

In 1913, the Japanese American people in California were targeted by the Alien Land Law. This law said that since the Issei could not be legal citizens, they didn't have the right to own land in California. So, many Issei bought land in their American-born children's names. Japanese Americans could still lease land, but only for 3 years. Two other states, Washington and Oregon, passed similar land laws.

In 1920, California passed the Amended Alien Land Law. The new law didn't allow any Issei to buy or rent land, either for themselves or under the names of their children who were American citizens.

Congress passed the Cable Act in 1922, which said that any American woman who married a new immigrant could lose her own citizenship. If the marriage ended because of death or divorce, a white woman of European descent could regain her American citizenship, but a Japanese American woman who was a citizen could not.

Two years later, Congress passed the Immigration Act of 1924. This act said that no more Asian immigrants could come to America. It stopped more Japanese from legally coming to the United States to live. People in Japan got very angry, and Japan's relationship with the United States started to head in the wrong direction. Japanese Americans were angry that their 14th Amendment rights were being ignored. This amendment states that no law can be passed that discriminates against a person on the basis of race, color, or creed. Nevertheless, the Immigration Act didn't change until 1952.

## WORLD WAR II (1939–1945)

In 1931, Japan was preparing to take over Asia by force. The Japanese people needed more living space, food, and raw materials such as oil, metal, and rubber. President Franklin D. Roosevelt wanted to stop Japan. By 1941, Japan and the United States had broken off business relations. As a warning to Japan, President Roosevelt stationed battleships at Pearl Harbor, a U.S. naval base in Hawaii. The commander of the Japanese Navy thought that a surprise attack would greatly hurt the U.S. Navy, and that Japan would then be free to take over Asia.

On December 7, 1941, the Japanese Imperial Forces bombed Pearl Harbor. The fears many Americans felt about anyone of Japanese descent grew stronger. Many Americans didn't trust the Japanese at all. On December 8, the U.S. Congress declared war on Japan. Within hours, the FBI arrested 736 Japanese people in Hawaii and on the U.S. mainland—they feared these people might be spies and help the enemy. In the first few days after the bombing of Pearl Harbor, nearly 1,400 Japanese Americans were put in jail by the government. These were mostly Issei community leaders, including teachers, priests, and newspaper editors.

The war got larger and more dangerous as the Axis Powers (Germany, Italy, and Japan) fought against the Allies (Great

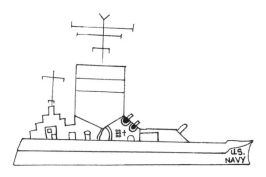

Britain, the Soviet Union, the United States, and 73 other nations). Prejudice against the Japanese in America grew. On January 5, 1942, about a month after the U.S. entered the war, the War Department said Japanese American men couldn't volunteer for the U.S. Army. The War Department thought that Japanese American men— even if they wanted to be in the Army— were America's enemies. Those who were already in the U.S. military were kicked out or demoted.

A lieutenant commander named Kenneth Duval Ringle was assigned to learn all he could about Japanese American loyalty. The report he wrote—as well as other secret reports written by the Navy—stated that Japanese Americans were loyal citizens of the United States. The reports argued that mass internment of Japanese Americans was not necessary. (Internment means keeping people confined, usually against their will, in an area or a camp.) Despite Mr. Ringle's report, President Franklin D. Roosevelt signed Executive Order 9066 on February 19, 1942, giving the Secretary of War the power to put any person thought to be a threat to the United States in an internment camp. In all, about 110,000 Japanese Americans were sent to internment camps during World War II. Almost 75,000 of these people were U.S. citizens.

## INTERNMENT CAMPS

In American history books, several names are used to describe the places where Japanese Americans were sent during World War II. The places set up by the War Relocation Authority were called "relocation camps." The Justice Department ran "internment camps," like the one in Crystal City, Texas, that were separate from the relocation camps. The War Relocation Authority also set up camps called "citizen isolation centers" near Leup, Arizona, and Moab, Utah. These centers were for people the government thought were troublemakers. Other people called these centers "detention camps." As early as October 20, 1942, President Roosevelt and other high-ranking government officials called all of these places "concentration camps."

The authors of this book decided not to use the term "concentration camps." This is out of respect for the millions of Jewish people and others who were killed in Nazi concentration camps in Germany during World War II. But most Japanese Americans feel that the names "relocation camps" and "detention camps" don't describe the hardship, shame, and loss of freedom they experienced. For these reasons, we chose to use the name "internment camps" in this book.

*This map shows many of the places where Japanese people were held during World War II. Japanese people who lived in the area that is shaded were ordered to move to an internment camp. The names in small letters were "assembly centers." The two names with a dot next to them were "citizen isolation centers." The names in big letters were permanent internment camps.*

When Executive Order 9066 went into effect, Japanese people on the West Coast were put under a curfew for a few months, then ordered to "evacuate" within a week. The curfew was a law that said that Japanese Americans couldn't be on the street after a certain time. The police put anyone who looked Japanese in jail if they broke the curfew, even if they were loyal American citizens.

The order to "evacuate" meant that Japanese Americans had to leave their homes and go to one of 16 "assembly centers" in California, Washington, Oregon, and Arizona. These centers were in places like horse racetracks and fairgrounds, and people had to live in them for 1 to 8 months while the internment camps were being built. While they were in the centers, the Japanese Americans were not told what was going to happen to them or even where they were going.

Some people moved to other states, out of the boundaries the government had set up, to escape being sent to a camp. Military leaders felt more threatened by Japanese Americans on the West Coast, because 95 percent of Japanese Americans lived there. After Pearl Harbor, their increasing numbers frightened others. But while some Japanese Americans left the West Coast, most stayed and followed orders to evacuate. Many were afraid they would be imprisoned if they disobeyed. Some peo-

ple lost everything they owned, including their businesses, cars, houses, and possessions. They could only take what they could carry with them to the camps.

In the last months of 1942, Japanese Americans were sent to one of ten permanent internment camps. These camps were in California, Arizona, Utah, Idaho, Wyoming, Colorado, and Arkansas. Some camps, like the one in Tule Lake, California, held 18,000 people—that's as many as a medium-sized town. Some were smaller, like the one in Granada, Colorado, which had 7,000 people. One of the Justice Department internment camps was in Crystal City, Texas, where Japanese Americans and others who were thought to be spies were sent.

All of this cost the U.S. government a lot of money, and yet there was never any proof that Japanese Americans weren't loyal American citizens. All the camps were located in isolated areas, away from other people. The people were always being watched from towers by guards with guns in their hands. It was enough to scare anyone! The years spent in the camps made many Japanese Americans feel guilty for things they did not do and left them feeling frustrated.

Conditions in the internment camps were awful. People lived in long, barrack-style, tar-papered buildings surrounded by barbed wire. There were 12 to 14 barracks in a block, and a total of 250 to 300 people lived in a single block. Each barrack had about six rooms. A whole family had to live in one room, and there might be as many as eight people in a family. Sometimes small families had to share a room with another family. The rooms were small, cramped, and dirty. In some, the walls didn't go all the way up to the ceiling. Everybody could hear everything that went on in the building.

One of the worst things about the housing was that family members did not have privacy inside their own room. People

sometimes hung blankets on a rope to make separate rooms. Even bathrooms were not private and had to be shared by everyone. People felt very uncomfortable and crowded, living with no privacy in such a large group of people. Can you imagine living under such conditions?

The people in the internment camps tried to entertain themselves by forming sewing and craft classes, and playing sports like baseball. Sometimes they drew pictures and wrote poetry and stories about life in the camps. They did this because they were not allowed to bring their cameras to take pictures that would show what happened in the camps.

The food at the camps was not the greatest—in fact, it was terrible! The same thing was often served day after day. At Poston, an internment camp in Arizona, dinner was sometimes potato hash and moldy bread.

The weather was a big concern, too. Since the barracks were poorly built, the cracks let in the dirt and rain. Can you imagine sweeping your room every time the wind blew? At many of the camps, the summer brought temperatures of more than 100 degrees in the shade, and the winters were freezing cold.

The adults did many things to make their new homes better. They built sports fields and schools. They raised chickens and grew vegetables. They did everything they could to make life as comfortable as possible.

After several months, each camp started

a school for the children. All of the teachers taught American history and the Pledge of Allegiance. We think it is amazing that Japanese Americans were forced to salute the American flag and pledge their loyalty to a country whose government had put them and their parents into internment camps.

Not many people know this, but in Hawaii, there were two internment camps, called Sand Island and Honouliuli. There were more than 160,000 people of Japanese descent in Hawaii, many more than in any state on the U.S. mainland. But the government did not order a major evacuation in Hawaii. More than 1,500 people were arrested in Hawaii, and 1,250 of them were eventually sent to one of the camps. But they were all given a hearing, which is a chance to defend yourself in court. Some people were allowed to go back to their homes. The Japanese Americans on the mainland were never given a hearing.

The reason that people living in Hawaii were treated differently from people living on the West Coast was that businesses in Hawaii depended on the Japanese Americans for labor and customers. If all people in Hawaii of Japanese descent had been put into camps, many stores would have gone out of business, and the owners of sugar cane fields would not have had enough laborers. Because the Japanese Americans in Hawaii were not all rounded up and sent to internment camps, the Nisei men from Hawaii were the first Japanese Americans to volunteer to serve their country in the U.S. Army.

In September 1945, the U.S. government decided it was no longer necessary to hold Japanese Americans in the internment camps. The Japanese Americans in the camps were told to leave the camps and return home, even if they no longer had homes to go to.

## SERVING OUR COUNTRY

In 1942, some Japanese Americans in the armed services were kicked out. Many pushed for the reopening of the draft to prove their loyalty to America, while other Japanese Americans didn't want to fight until they had their rights restored. The government realized that having interpreters who could speak

Japanese was important, so the ban was lifted in 1943.

While many Japanese Americans spent World War II in internment camps, others left the camps to risk their lives fighting for their country. During the war, Japanese Americans served in the 442nd Regimental Combat Team, the Military Intelligence Service, the 100th Battalion, the 552nd Field Artillery Battalion, and the Women's Army Corps. Many women also served in the army as nurses or translators. By the

World Times News

Most Decorated Team

442nd Combat Team of all Japanese Americans have won more medals and decorations than any other military unit in American history.

end of World War II, more than 33,000 Nisei had served in the armed forces.

On February 1, 1943, the 442nd Regimental Combat Team was created. About 4,500 Japanese American men came from the mainland and Hawaii to join. They trained for the Army at Camp Shelby in Mississippi. These soldiers fought many battles during World War II. The most famous ones were in France, one in the town of Bruyeres and one called the "Battle of the Lost Battalion," where Japanese American soldiers rescued a squad of fighting men from Texas. About 1,000 Japanese American soldiers died or were

hurt trying to rescue 250 men.

The Japanese American 442nd Regimental Combat Team became famous because they won more medals and decorations than any other military unit of their size in American history. They fought for their country even though their moms, dads, wives, and children were behind barbed wire in the internment camps. One man named Sadao Munemori won the Medal of Honor, because he threw himself on a hand grenade to save two of the men in his platoon.

Many people don't know this, but the men in the 552nd Field Artillery were among the first Allied troops to rescue prisoners from Dachau, a German concentration camp. Many of the prisoners in the camp were sick, starving, or dying. The Japanese American soldiers were told not to give the prisoners food, clothes, or medical help, but they did anyway. They were told not to talk about the rescue, so they never got credit for being at Dachau. Most history books do not mention their actions, either.

The U.S. government asked other Japanese Americans who could speak, read, and write Japanese to fight for America by being interpreters. These Japanese Americans were in the Military Intelligence Service (MIS). Many of the men and women in the MIS had to work for America while their families were in the internment camps, too. The work they did was really secret, and for many years, no one knew about them or about what kind of work they did to help in World War II.

The war ended when President Harry Truman ordered the military to bomb the Japanese cities of Nagasaki (nah-gah-sah-kee) and Hiroshima (hee-roh-shee-mah) in August 1945. This was the first time in history that atomic bombs were used, and it changed the world forever. Many Japanese Americans were glad the war was finally over, but they were also very sad because they had relatives who were hurt or killed in the bombings. Some Japanese Americans in the MIS were sent to Nagasaki and Hiroshima to translate for the people who survived the bombings.

## CHALLENGING THE U.S. GOVERNMENT

When Japanese Americans were put under a curfew in 1942, some people protested. Many people said that the curfew was unconstitutional, that it took away rights guaranteed by the U.S. Constitution.

Four people who were put in jail for breaking curfew were Gordon Hirabayashi, Minoru Yasui, Fred Korematsu, and Mitsuye Endo. They went to court to fight for their rights, but they lost their cases. Many years after the war, these people went to court again because they felt they had been unjustly convicted. They had been put in camps, but they hadn't done anything wrong. Mitsuye Endo won her case in 1944—the court decided she was a loyal citizen and let her out of the camp.

Another group of people who challenged the U.S. government were some Nisei men from the Heart Mountain camp near Cody, Wyoming. They did not want to be drafted into the army until their constitutional rights were given back to them. They said they would agree to be drafted if their families were let out of the camps. The government said no to this. Some of the men who didn't want to be drafted had to go to prison for 3 years because they stood up for their rights.

## AFTER WORLD WAR II

Over time, the government and the American people began to see that the Japanese Americans had been unfairly treated during World War II. In 1948, President Truman signed the Japanese American Evacuation Claims Act, which promised to pay Japanese Americans back for what they

*A large group of Japanese people becoming American citizens*

Courtesy of Archie A. Miyatake

had lost when they were sent to the camps. But the act said that they needed to show exact records proving what they had lost. Most did not have any records, and besides, the hard work they had put into building a farm or a business could never be paid back with money. Other Japanese Americans felt that the government should repay them not only with money but with an apology, too.

When they left the camps, the Japanese Americans had a hard time starting over, because they had lost so much money, property, and time. The average age of an Issei woman after the war was 47. The average age of an Issei man was 55, and the average age of a Nisei child was 17. It was almost impossible to make enough money to buy what they needed to start all over. But like other Americans, Japanese Americans believed in hard work, honesty, independence, and not giving up. These beliefs helped them go back to their communities and build their lives again.

After World War II, many Japanese Americans and Issei went to court to make Congress understand that treating them like foreigners—sometimes even enemies—

was not constitutional. Congress was convinced. In 1952, it passed an act called the McCarran-Walter Immigration and Naturalization Act. This act allowed Japanese Issei to become American citizens for the first time. Soon after this act was passed, thousands of Issei became citizens of the United States.

Even though many Japanese Americans had college educations, they still had a hard time getting jobs and buying homes, because some Americans were still prejudiced. The Issei were allowed to work in any business they were qualified for, but only within the Japanese American community. Yet, by the late 1960s, because of their hard work, many Nisei and Sansei

*A Japanese American family stands in front of their restaurant*

were just as well off as white Americans of European descent.

The Japanese American struggle was hard on the Issei. They were having a hard time living the way they had lived before the internment camps of World War II. Some of the Nisei spoke out about their hard times, but most were quiet and did not want to talk about their life in the camps. The Sansei helped the Nisei talk about the camps and their experiences. Many of the Sansei wanted Japanese Americans to tell their story to the public and to fight for their constitutional rights. The Sansei felt that most Americans believed Japanese Americans to be quiet and obedient, and they wanted to change this stereotype.

Many Sansei never learned to speak, read, or write Japanese. It's sad that they lost this part of their heritage, and it made many Issei feel cut off from their grandchildren. Some Sansei are now starting to learn the Japanese language.

## REDRESS

In the 1960s, many minorities, including Japanese Americans, began looking back into their histories. They wanted to learn more about themselves, to find out who they were and where their beliefs came from. Martin Luther King Jr., who led the civil rights movement for African-Americans, and Cesar Chavez, who led the migrant farm workers in California, were two men who inspired Japanese Americans to fight for their own rights.

Japanese Americans studied the history of World War II and realized how unfairly their people had been treated. In the 1970s, many Japanese Americans felt that they should do something about it. They wanted the U.S. government to apologize to the Japanese Americans for what had happened during the war, and to recognize that they took away the Japanese Americans' constitutional rights. They called this action "redress," which means "to correct" or "to repay." It wasn't the money that the Sansei wanted, but an apology. Another goal of redress was to teach people about what had happened to Japanese Americans, so that it would never happen again to anyone.

In 1980, President Jimmy Carter ordered a group of officials to study the internment camps and Executive Order 9066. This group decided that the Japanese Americans had been treated unfairly and should get both an apology and money. Many Japanese American organizations got together to work on getting a bill passed in Congress. Other people besides Japanese Americans also helped. The cases of Hirabayashi, Yasui, and Korematsu were also being retried around the same time, so a lot of attention was paid to this bill. The bill

THE WHITE HOUSE
WASHINGTON

A monetary sum and words alone cannot restore lost years or
erase painful memories; neither can they fully convey our Nation's
resolve to rectify injustice and to uphold the rights of individuals.
We can never fully right the wrongs of the past.  But we can take a
clear stand for justice and recognize that serious injustices were
done to Japanese Americans during World War II.

In enacting a law calling for restitution and offering a sincere
apology, your fellow Americans have, in a very real sense, renewed
their traditional commitment to the ideals of freedom, equality, and
justice.  You and your family have our best wishes for the future.

Sincerely,

GEORGE BUSH
PRESIDENT OF THE UNITED STATES

OCTOBER 1990

*A letter from President George Bush apologizing for the U.S. government's treatment of Japanese
Americans during World War II*

was called the Civil Liberties Act of 1988, and it was signed by President Ronald Reagan. By passing this act, the U.S. government admitted that it had made a mistake in putting Japanese Americans into internment camps and paid them a sum of money. The first letter of apology was signed by President George Bush in 1990. As you can see, it took a long time.

Some Japanese Americans were happy when they received their letter of apology and the money. Others didn't want anything. They just wanted to forget their experiences in the camps. For others, the money helped, although it could never repay them for their years in the camps, and the apology helped them to believe again in the U.S. Constitution. Today, many people spend time discussing what happened to Japanese Americans in World War II.

## CONCLUSION

Even though the Japanese Americans got money and an apology for what was done to them during World War II, they still face racism and prejudice. We hope this book helps people understand what happened to the Japanese Americans, so that no one is treated unfairly because of where they came from, how they look, what language they speak, or what they believe. We hope that all people are treated equally and given their constitutional rights.

We have learned that the Issei tried to make a good life in America. They put up with a lot of hardship so that their children would have a better life. This is why most immigrants come to the United States. The Nisei tried to fit into their new culture and home, but they also wanted to keep their traditional Japanese ways alive. Many Nisei were not told about their parents' experiences. Today, the Sansei and Yonsei—the third and fourth generations—have had time to think about these events. They want to learn as much as possible about their heritage, culture, and history. They also want to share what they know, because Japanese American history is a part of American history.

# OUR FAMILIES' STORIES

*It's fun to look back through your family tree,*
*And learn about your grandparents' history.*
*Picture brides, internment camps, and stories galore.*
*Things from the past, to learn and explore.*

Here we share the stories of our grandparents. Each one is very special to us. These stories will help you understand the lives of people who came before us.

### Grandpa's Letter
**by Zeni Whittall**

When I was in the sixth grade, my class studied World War II. There was no reference to the Japanese American internment camps in our history books. I wanted people to know what had happened to thousands of Japanese Americans less than 50 years ago, because I am half–Japanese American. I wrote a letter to my grandfather and asked him if he would tell me about what happened.

This letter is the only time that my grandfather shared his story with anyone in my

*Zeni Whittall with his grandfather*

family in writing. My grandfather was Nisei Japanese American. Many times before, my mother had asked him what had happened in the camp, but because of the pain and the shame, he could not share it with her. Many other Japanese Americans who were interned have not shared their painful memories with their children, either. After reparations from the government, however, they are now finding the strength to tell their grandchildren.

I'm sharing this letter with you because I want this to be remembered. My grandfather can never tell his story again, because he has passed away. So read this and remember what has happened, and never let it happen again:

*Dear Zeni,*

*I'll be glad to give you a brief outline of my experience during our relocation from the West Coast by the U.S. government.*

*As I recall, we were living on a small truck farm in Dominguez, California. About March or April of 1942, my dad, mother, little sister, and I were told to pack everything that we could into my dad's car, and go to San Pedro. From there we drove "caravan style" with military escorts to Santa Anita racetrack in Arcadia. This was called Santa Anita Assembly Center.*

*Once there, my dad's car was taken and sold. We were directed to the stable area, where we filled bags with straw for mattresses. The stable area became our home for the next six months. We ate in army style "mess halls" and took community showers. Since I was ten years old, I had*

*to go to school, which was set up in the grandstands. The adults, though, were put to work making camouflage nets.*

*About September 1942, we were moved by train to Jerome, Arkansas. The total trip took over a week, and the whole way we were guarded by military police. The drapes on the train were drawn the whole trip, and we were forbidden to look out. The camp was in a remote area away from anything. There were guard towers and the whole camp was fenced with barbed wire. I remember all the different wildlife: poisonous snakes, fireflies, and flying squirrels. The weather was hot and humid in the summer, but in the winter it was cold and even snowed on occasion.*

*While in the camp I got to join the Boy Scouts, and my troop was able to go out to be with other troops during jamborees. During all of this, I was too young to really know what was going on, so I just had fun. I would play games with the other kids in camp, and we had the great outdoors. I guess it was just like a very long summer.*

*Around July or August of 1944, we moved to another camp in Gila River, Arizona. What a contrast to Arkansas—first a hot, humid climate and then a desert. While here, my dad left camp to go to work in Idaho. Later he was preparing to send for us, but my mom wanted to be anything but a part of Idaho. Since the order that banned us from the West Coast was lifted, my mom made arrangements for us to return to California.*

*About September 1945, we were back in Los Angeles. We were very fortunate because the people my father leased his farm from before the war were very kind. They helped my dad get back on his feet by giving us some furnishings.*

*You asked me how I felt about what happened then and now. As I said before, I was pretty young when all of this hap-pened. I didn't know what it was all about, except the fact that America and Japan were at war. I met a lot of people, shared many experiences, and overall I don't think that it scared me all that much. Today I feel very sad for all of the older people like my dad and also the college students. They knew it was wrong and they fought for more than 40 years to get the U.S. government to acknowledge the mistake that had been imposed on thousands, the forceful relocation of the Japanese Americans from the coast.*

*In October of 1988, President Ronald Reagan signed the Civil Liberties Act of 1988, which was the formal apology to all of the Japanese Americans who had been interned during World War II.*

*Love, Grandpa*

Chris Tucker

*A monument honoring Governor Ralph Carr in Sakura Square in Denver*

## My Grandpa's Story
### by Harold Sampson Jr.

After Franklin Roosevelt signed Executive Order 9066, some of my relatives had to leave California or be put in internment camps. However, Grandfather's family had a choice. They could go to an internment camp or move to Colorado, where they would be free. They decided to move out.

They traveled by caravan (one car, two pickups, and one truck) through Arizona and New Mexico. As they drove through towns and cities, people threw trash and garbage at them. They were not allowed to stop and rest. They were escorted by the state police through the states of Arizona and New Mexico, and were only allowed to buy gas for the car and hamburgers to eat.

When they got to the border of Colorado, a state patrolman met them and said, "Welcome to Colorado. Governor Ralph Carr and the people of Colorado welcome you. Is there anything I can help you with?" Governor Carr had sent this patrolman to meet the caravan and offer them help. He was a great man and the only governor to welcome the Japanese Americans to his state. This is why the Japanese American community built a special monument for Governor Carr in the beautiful garden at Sakura Square in Denver.

## Grandpa Ozaki's Story
### by Meg Ozaki

This is a story of my grandpa, Motoichi Ozaki, or Joe M. Ozaki, who was born and lived in Shingu, Wakayama Ken, Japan. At the age of 20, Grandpa moved to Peru with his cousin for a better job. They lived with their aunt and uncle for a year. Grandpa got a job selling cloth, stockings, and underwear. Working at the store was an exciting experience. Once he had to stay up all night and guard it with a gun to protect it from looters. He worked there for 3 years and then quit. When Grandpa's aunt and uncle went back to Japan, he took over their flooring business.

In 1940, Tamiye Saki—Grandpa's arranged wife—came from Japan to marry him. They

*Meg Ozaki with her grandfather, Motoichi "Joe" Ozaki*

celebrated with a few close friends. Their first child was born on May 21, 1942. They named him Francisco Kuniaki Ozaki. He is my father.

Grandpa recalls the day he learned of the bombing of Pearl Harbor. He and grandma were driving to Lima from the beach listening to the car radio, when a news flash interrupted the music and told of the attack. From then on, things started changing slowly. First, detectives started making lists of Japanese business workers in Lima. Then the government passed a law forbidding any Japanese to go more than 5 miles away from the city. After that, Grandpa's business slowed down, and he started losing employees. Finally, in February of 1943, Peruvian detectives took him from Lima to a government detention center.

The next morning, Grandpa was taken to Crystal City, an internment camp near San Antonio, Texas. Peru shipped all the Japanese in the country to internment camps in the U.S. Grandma and my father joined him 6 months later.

During the long years in camp, Grandpa helped write a Japanese newspaper. The people were allowed to bring only $300 per person when they came to the camp. Grandpa's family used all their money on food.

In the camp, the family grew. Two baby girls were born, and Grandpa's father, who had been living in an internment camp in Santa Fe, New Mexico, was sent to Crystal City at Grandpa's request.

Grandpa had the freedom he had in Peru taken away from him, but his philosophy was still to make the best of things. After the war was over, his family stayed in the camp until it was ready to close. Peru had told him not to come back, because he wasn't a citizen. The only places in the United States that would accept the Peruvian Japanese were Seabrook Farms in New Jersey and the state of Colorado.

Grandpa found relatives in Colorado and took his family there. He has lived there since September of 1946.

## My Grandma's Story
### by Dara Domoto

My grandma's head throbbed with worry when she read the newspaper headline: "U.S. Drops Atomic Bomb on Hiroshima and Nagasaki: Japan Surrenders!" Grandma Domoto thought immediately of her family who lived near Hiroshima. Did they get hurt? Were they alive? She had not been able to write to them since the beginning of World War II, when she

*Dara Domoto reading a story with Grandma Domoto*

My great-grandma Kinoshita, who lived in Colorado, found out that most of her family in Nagasaki were all right, except that one of her nine brothers and sisters was killed in the war. Even though she had family in Japan, great-Grandma still felt that her own sons should fight for the United States. She was proud when two of her sons joined the armed services.

Our family was lucky that many of our relatives survived a very sad time.

We learned a lot talking to our grandparents and writing a part of our family's history. You might want to do this for your family, too. It would make a nice present to give to someone you love.

and grandpa were sent from California to an internment camp in Colorado. They lived in the camp for 4 years. Can you imagine how terrible it would be, not knowing about your family for that long?

After the war, my grandparents were let out of camp and went back to California, only to discover that all their stored belongings were gone. One good thing did happen, though. Grandma got a letter from her family telling her they were all right. Her brother told her that he biked into Hiroshima from their farm a couple days after the bombing. He was sad to see people suffering, with maggots and flies in their open wounds. There wasn't enough medicine to treat everyone. It must have been a terrible sight.

*Dara's great-grandma Kinoshita and her son Carl*

# CULTURE AND THE ARTS

*Culture is fun for everyone.*
*The sounds of music and the beauty in art,*
*The festivals people celebrate,*
*All these customs show what's in the heart.*

This chapter tells you about Japanese American cultural arts and festivals. Japanese Americans enjoy the beauty of art, the rhythm of music, and the joy of dancing, especially at celebrations and festivals, where the people come together as a community. Many Americans from other backgrounds also enjoy these parts of Japanese American culture.

We discovered that the qualities of calmness, patience, concentration, and determination are important to all of these activities. In this chapter, we feature some talented artists, some awesome "moves" in the martial arts, and recommend some cool music.

## FESTIVALS

*On New Year's Day carps wave from the poles,*
*And rice is always in the bowls!*
*We liked these festivals and holidays,*
*We learned about them in many ways.*

### Oshogatsu

New Year's Day, or *Oshogatsu* (oh-shoh-gaht-soo), is celebrated on January 1 by many Japanese Americans across our nation. It is the most important, festive,

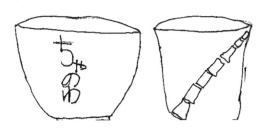

and memorable occasion of the year. It is a time for special decorations, food, and traditions. The Japanese American New Year's celebration, including the decorating, cleaning, cooking, and visiting, all came from Japan. But it's slightly different in our country, because it has become a mixture of Japanese tradition and American customs.

Since food is such an important part of this celebration, families prepare special foods like carp, which represents determination, and *soba* noodles, which represent long life. They also cook *daikon*, a Japanese radish, which represents happiness; *mochi*, sweet rice balls that represent good fortune; *kombu*, seaweed that represents happiness; *kuro mame* (koo-roh mah-meh), which represents good health; black beans that represent good luck; and *sake*, rice wine. At the end of each year, people eat a bowl of *soba*, which is buckwheat noodle soup. Soba noodles stand for money and riches, and are a lucky charm.

*Mochi tsuki*—making sweet rice balls— is a special part of the New Year's celebration. Today in Japan, mochi tsuki is done by rural families and temples. Japanese American candy stores, bakeries, families and groups get together to make and eat mochi.

Another tradition that is still followed by Japanese Americans is cleaning. Cooking and house cleaning are done before the first few days of the New Year have begun. The idea is to start the new year with a clean slate. If you owe people money, you should pay it at this time. Also,

personal problems should be solved. *Bonen kai* (boh-nehn kye), year-end parties, are given by companies, clubs, and friends to encourage friendships and to wish each other good luck.

On Oshogatsu, many Japanese Americans get up early and wish each family member, "Happy New Year!" In Japanese, you would say, "*Shinnen Akemashite Omedetto Gozaimasu*," pronounced "sheen-nehn ah-keh-mahsh-teh oh-meh-deh-toh goh-zy-ee-mahs." Everyone dresses up in new clothes and visits friends and relatives. They enjoy eating *ozoni*, a soup with pieces of mochi (pounded rice cake), vegetables, and fish. Ozoni represents a long and good life.

### Hina Matsuri

*Hina Matsuri* (hee-nah maht-soo-ree) means "Girls' Day." It is a day when families honor girls, in Japan and America. Hina Matsuri is on March 3 of each year. In Japan, the peach blossoms bloom in the spring. They represent happiness in marriage to Japanese American women.

Families in Japan and the United States want their daughters to grow up and have happy lives. Parents in Japan want their daughters to be happy by having good marriages. They celebrate Girls' Day to teach their daughters how to be good wives who are kind, gentle, and peaceful. In America, Japanese American families want their daughters to choose their own lives, which could mean career, marriage, or a combination of both.

When Japanese Americans celebrate Hina Matsuri, they follow the examples set by their grandparents and show respect for their culture by observing the day. Some Japanese Americans display special Japanese dolls on Hina Matsuri.

Girls display the dolls that are most important to them. The very precious dolls called *Hina Ningyo*, or "miniature dolls," represent the Imperial Court of Japan from 300 years ago. These dolls are dressed in kimonos and are surrounded by miniature horns, dressers, chairs, tables, pictures, and other tiny household things. They are displayed on a *hina-dan*, a doll stand, which is covered with a red cloth. The hina-dan has five to seven tiers, or steps, built into it. The dolls are arranged by their place of honor, so the Emperor and Empress are on the top. The Imperial Court sets are rare and expensive, so few Japanese Americans own them.

Some people display their dolls in their home, or at a church or community center. If it is a large celebration, one or more sets of the Imperial Court dolls and other valuable Japanese dolls might be displayed in a large room. When Japanese Americans display their dolls, they want to teach others about Japanese culture, so they might also prepare Japanese food for the visitors to enjoy.

## Tango No Sekku

May 5 is *Tango No Sekku* (tahn-goh noh seh-koo), the annual Boys' Day festival in the Japanese American community. On this day, families with one or more sons put up bamboo flagpoles in their yards. From the poles they hang carp (fish) kites or wind socks. (We tell you how to make a wind sock in the Hands-On Fun chapter.) Carps stand for bravery, strength, and determination—qualities that families want their sons to have. The biggest carp

wind sock represents the oldest son and the smallest carp represents the youngest son. The wind socks are hollow, and when the wind blows and fills the inside, the fish seem to be swimming. Some carp kites or wind socks are more than 8 feet long.

Inside the house, many families display warrior dolls, armor, helmets, and other things that represent strength. As you can see, strength is a very important quality for boys in Japanese American culture. These objects are very expensive and detailed, so they are displayed only on important days.

In Japan, the boys often bathe in water that has been soaked in the leaves of the iris plant. The leaves are shaped like a sword and also stand for strength. Boys also eat a special meal of rice wrapped in the leaves of iris, bamboo, or oak, for good luck and, of course, strength. This part of the custom is not usually fol-

lowed here in America. It is only practiced in Japan.

We would like you to know a little of the history of Boys' Day. According to an ancient Japanese legend, one day a boy named Kintaro stood beside a river, watching some fishermen. Suddenly, he saw a man-eating carp swimming toward the men. The fishermen didn't notice the carp, so Kintaro jumped into the river. He fought with the fish and killed it. Ever since then, on May 5, the festival of Boys' Day—now called Children's Day—has been celebrated in Japan.

In Japan, you see many colorful carp kites and wind socks flying, because Boys' Day is such a big festival. Tango No Sekku is not as popular in America, because it falls on the same day as Cinco de Mayo (The Fifth of May), a day celebrated by

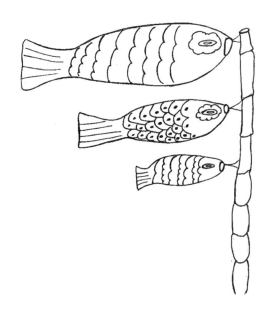

Hispanics. If you want to celebrate both cultures, you could fly your carp wind sock, eat somen noodles, and display your warrior dolls, as well as hit piñatas and eat tostadas.

## Obon

*Obon* (oh-bohn), or *Bon*, is a festival for Buddhists to welcome the spirits of the dead. It's kind of like Memorial Day. Obon is also called "the Festival of Lanterns" because colorful lanterns are displayed.

Japanese Americans observe Obon between July 15 and August 15. Obon has become a part of Japanese American culture and is certainly one of the most colorful festivals of the year. For people who are Buddhist, Obon is a time to pay respect to the Buddhist way of life. They look back upon the love, affection, compassion, and qualities that their parents and others who have died gave them while they lived.

Japanese American Buddhists celebrate Obon with a service. Although it is a memorial service, a festive mood exists. People wear light, colorful summer cotton kimonos called *yukata*. The importance of Obon is to teach *kansha*, which is gratitude toward parents and ancestors. It also stresses the importance of *dana*, or selfless giving, which should be practiced by family members, close friends, and, of course, all of us.

During this celebration, people gather in the streets and the temples to dance. *Bon-Odori*, an Obon dance, is a dance of rejoicing for the gifts of relatives who have died. These folk dances are rhythmic and simple. The young and old dance together.

Obon is celebrated in both large and small cities that have Japanese American Buddhist communities, including San Francisco, Chicago, New York, Seattle, Denver, and Honolulu. It has become a community activity where both Buddhists and Christians celebrate and remember their Japanese roots together.

## Sakura Matsuri

In March or April, the Japanese people celebrate a change of the season. They go to the mountains to see the *sakura* — the cherry blossoms—and picnic with their friends. The short life of the sakura adds a sadness to their beauty. For this reason, the Japanese see them as more important than other flowers.

Many years ago, the Japanese government presented some cherry trees to the

United States as a gift. Now, every April, many Japanese Americans and other people visit Washington, D.C., to participate in the Cherry Blossom Festival. Many communities in the United States have Cherry Blossom Festivals. It has become a time for Japanese Americans to gather with friends and family, and share their culture and food through demonstrations, parades, food bazaars, and carnivals.

*A Nisei Week parade in Los Angeles*

## Nisei Week

One of the largest Japanese American festivals in the United States is called Nisei Week. It is celebrated in Little Tokyo in Los Angeles, California.

The first Nisei Week was held August 12–18, 1934. That year, the Nisei wanted the Issei to attract business back to Little Tokyo. They wanted more people to work and to do their shopping in Little Tokyo, because the Great Depression had hurt everyone's business. They decided to hold a big festival to attract business to Little Tokyo. The Nisei held a beauty contest and a baby contest, and had a parade with Japanese American groups like Girl and Boy Scouts, bowling and baseball teams, floats, and dancers in kimonos.

Nisei Week is still celebrated today and includes Japanese American art exhibits and demonstrations, a fashion show, baby contests, martial arts contests, banquets honoring Issei pioneers, a carnival, a beauty contest, and a parade. It is such a big celebration that it is on television in Los Angeles. Some of the grand marshals of the parade have been famous people,

such as the movie star Noriyuki "Pat" Morita, Hawaiian Senator Daniel Inouye, and other celebrities. Nisei Week is a time for Japanese Americans to gather and show pride in their heritage.

## Kenjinkai Picnic

If you had come to America 100 years ago from Japan, you might have gotten homesick. One way the Issei solved this problem was to stay in contact with other immigrants from their *ken*, or home state in Japan. This helped people forget their loneliness for friends and family in Japan.

A very important community event started by Japanese Americans was the annual picnic, where people from different kenjinkai joined together in celebration. There were games and races for the children and adults. Singers, dancers, and bands playing Japanese music entertained everyone. Often, picnickers would get on stage and sing traditional folk songs.

People brought a packed lunch, called an *obento*, to the picnic in a special three-layer lacquered box set. The set was wrapped with a *furoshiki*, a scarf that had a Japanese design. Each layer was arranged in a pretty way. Some foods that were included were *onigiri*, rice balls; *tsukemono*, pickled vegetables; *teriyaki* chicken; *sashimi*, raw fish; *nishime*, a one-pot vegetable dish; and *tempura*, deep-fried vegetables or seafood. The lunch was shared by friends and relatives. Kenjinkai picnics are still celebrated today.

## MARTIAL ARTS

Sometimes when we think of art, we think only about things that are on paper or things that we can make. We learned about an art that you can do! Martial arts are a fun and exciting way to get exercise and learn about yourself.

### Karate

There are many types of *karate* (kah-rah-teh). Karate is more than 300 years old. It is a type of self-defense that uses punching, kicking, and moving. In karate, you have to be quick. If someone throws a punch at you, you can dodge it or block it.

There are hundreds of stances in karate. We have drawn three basic stances (below), so you can see what they look like. They are the front stance, the back stance, and the horse. These are stances

Chris Tucker

*"Karate" means "the empty hand"*

every person in karate must know.

In karate, you wear a clean, white uniform and a belt, just as you do in judo. Each belt is a different color and stands for a different rank. The belt order is white, orange, yellow, blue, green, purple, brown, and black. In most groups, the black belt is the highest.

FRONT STANCE

BACK STANCE

HORSE STANCE

In karate, you practice by sparring. Sparring looks like fighting, but it is really a time to perfect your moves. You wear special pads to protect your fists and head. You can also use blocks in karate. Blocks

Chris Tucker

*Students demonstrating karate*

are ways to defend yourself with your arms and legs that stop your opponent from striking or kicking you.

A *kata* is several offensive and defensive movements put together. There are different katas, or forms. There is a kata for each belt. You need to know the kata and its meaning to pass the test for each belt. Your kata needs to be perfect before you can go on to the next higher belt.

Karate tournaments are held all across our country. At a tournament, you do your kata and then you free-spar in front of judges. The kata score can be from 0 to 10. Usually people score between 6 and 9. It is very unusual for people to get a perfect score. If you do well, you can get first, second, or third place.

We have told you about the exercise part, but we also want you to know that karate builds self-confidence and discipline. It teaches you to set goals and aim for them. The *sensei*, or teacher, stresses these things with his or her students.

So, if you would like to develop self-confidence, have fun, get exercise, and compete with an opponent, you should study karate. Karate is an exciting sport that uses the total mind and body.

## Judo

Did you know that *judo* (joo-doh) can save your life? Judo means "the gentle way." It is a form of wrestling, but it is not used for fighting. Instead, it teaches you ways to escape from danger. In judo, you learn how to fall safely so you won't get hurt or break any bones.

As in karate, you wear a white uniform that looks like a jacket with loose-fitting pants called a *gi*. You use a colored belt to hold your gi together. The color of the belt stands for a different rank; it is different depending on what school you go to. There are three levels in each color except black. The third level is *sankyu* (sahn-kyoo), the second level is *nikkyu* (nee-kyoo), and the first level is *ikkyu* (ee-kyoo). The highest color belt in judo is usually a black belt. There are ten *dans* (steps) in the black-belt rank, and ten is the highest. If you want to be a black belt, you have to show that you can do *Nage no Kata* (nah-geh noh kah-tah). These are a set of 15 different throws. You also have to show that you are a responsible person and that you will teach judo to other people.

When you begin to teach others judo, it is called *giri* (gee-ree), which means "obligation." You teach three things: self-defense, respect for nature, and discipline to your family, your friends, and people in your community.

Today, judo is an event in the Olympic games. We think judo is a good way to defend yourself when a lot of people try to gang up on you. Learning about judo makes us want to sign up.

## Kendo and Naginata

If you ever dreamed about being a famous martial artist, you will love learning about *kendo* (kehn-doh) and *naginata* (nah-gee-nah-tah). These two martial arts require you to really concentrate on what you are doing. Both are forms of self-defense and are also practiced in competition.

Many years ago, samurai warriors developed kendo to practice their sword-fighting skills. Today, kendo is a competitive sport studied here in the United States by men and women. Kendo means "the way of the sword." It is the Japanese style of fencing. A bamboo stick is used instead of a sword, and a steel grill is worn over the face like a mask. Arm coverings and a shoulder- and breastplate

made of painted bamboo are used to protect the body. A long skirt is also worn, so you can't tell which way the fencer's feet are moving.

We were lucky to meet and interview a woman who is an expert at naginata. Her name is Candy Tsutsui. Mrs. Tsutsui competes in many matches and has practiced many years to be a martial arts expert. Mrs. Tsutsui is very good at karate, but especially good at naginata. She uses some of the same techniques that the samurai warriors used in the old days. She has even been to Japan to compete in a tournament. For competitions, she dresses in a traditional outfit. Traditional protective gear can cost between $20,000 and $30,000! Luckily, there is a

way to make gear out of fiberglass, which costs less. Mrs. Tsutsui has strong, proud feelings about her heritage. She demonstrates this by keeping the old traditions alive.

Kendo and naginata are fun martial arts to watch, especially because of the fierce sounds the competitors make. We think it's neat that these martial arts are used for self-defense and competition, and not for fighting. Anyone can take lessons. Maybe you would like to try it.

## MUSIC AND DANCE

Another way you can learn about Japanese American culture is by listening to the music and watching the dances. In this section, you'll learn about some Japanese instruments, two Japanese American musical groups, and some Japanese ways of dancing and singing. This will give you a better understanding of the Japanese American heritage and help you appreciate different art forms.

## Taiko

*Taiko* (ty-koh) is an ancient form of drumming that was invented by a group of farmers long ago in Japan. The farmers used it to scare away any demons they thought would ruin their crops. After many years, it became a traditional folk art. Japanese Americans brought taiko to the United States.

*Students demonstrating taiko drumming*

Taiko consists of drums and percussion instruments that come in many shapes and sizes. The American-style taiko drums are made out of wine barrels and cowhides, while the other percussion instruments are made out of metal and wood. The music has a lot of different rhythms and patterns.

Vibrating drumbeats fill the air when a taiko group plays. The performances are very loud and exciting. They sound like thunder. The energy of the music adds to the excitement of the audience. The vibrations make you want to jump or pop and fly in the air.

There are many adult and children's taiko groups in Japanese American communities. Some of the authors of this book belong to a taiko group. People play the taiko drums because it's fun. They want to carry on the tradition so it won't be forgotten.

## Shakuhachi

The tone of the *shakuhachi* (shah-koo-hah-chee) is very soothing and calming. It makes you feel like you're in the woods. The instrument is long and made out of a bamboo stick with finger holes. You play it by blowing into it like a flute. It originated in China, like most other Japanese instruments. The shakuhachi is used in traditional Japanese music and modern American music. A well known Japanese

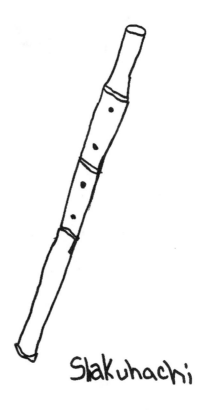

Shakuhachi

American jazz musician named Yutaka plays the shakuhachi.

## Koto

The word *koto* originally stood for "all kinds of string instruments." The koto is often referred to as the Japanese harp. The koto has 13 silk strings that pass over moveable bridges and are played with three "plectra" (like large guitar picks) worn on the thumb and two fingers. The koto is played flat on the floor, on your knees, or on a stand.

In the past, the koto was used only for classical Japanese music. But today, many modern Japanese American jazz groups use the koto when they play their music.

*Japanese women playing the koto*

The group Hiroshima uses this instrument. We liked the beautiful sounds of the koto.

## Samisen

Another traditional Japanese string instrument is the *samisen* (sah-mee-sehn). The first samisen was built in 1562. It is made of wood and has three strings and a wooden bridge. The covering is made of snakeskin. It looks almost like a banjo.

The samisen makes a high-pitched plucking sound. You play it like a guitar, sitting on your knees on the floor. It is played the traditional way, which is what you hear in classical Japanese music. It is also played the modern way, which is more of a jazz sound. It is played with a plectrum, which is like a guitar pick, or *bachi*, sticks used to strike the strings.

## MUSICAL GROUPS

We don't have room to talk about all the different groups that use these instruments, but we can tell you about two groups: One World Taiko and Hiroshima. We have chosen these two groups because they are two of the leaders in keeping Japanese American music alive.

### One World Taiko

We were lucky to have Nancy Ozaki and Gary Tsujimoto of One World Taiko perform for us. They take taiko drumming and

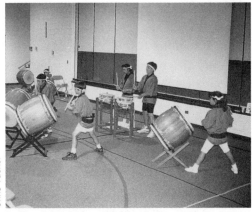

*Some of the authors playing taiko music*

Bob Hsiang

*Gary Tsujimoto and Nancy Ozaki of One World Taiko*

combine the sounds of many cultures of America with the sounds of their ancestors. When they play, it is almost as if they know each other's thoughts because they play together so perfectly.

Nancy Ozaki was born on Valentine's Day 1951 in Denver, Colorado, where she grew up. She is a second-generation Japanese American, or Nisei. As a teacher on a Navajo reservation, she was inspired by the Navajos' drums and music. She joined a Denver taiko group in 1976. In 1988, Ms. Ozaki moved to California and taught in an elementary school. She joined a taiko group there, too. This is where she met Gary Tsujimoto, a composer who also played taiko. Because they worked very well together, they started their own group. In 1989, they got married and moved to Pacifica, near San Francisco.

Mr. Tsujimoto was born in 1952 and is a third-generation Japanese America, or Sansei. When he was in his twenties, he began playing taiko. He liked taiko because

it combined his love of drums and karate with respect for his culture.

If you looked for the couple now, you would find them in Florida, working for Disney World at the EPCOT Center, sharing with others their love of taiko. Ms. Ozaki and Mr. Tsujimoto are very proud to be able to keep this part of their Japanese American heritage alive. We feel their name "One World Taiko" says it all—we all live in one world.

## Hiroshima

Hiroshima is a Sansei band that combines Japanese and American music together. The group plays music that sounds different to each person who listens. You might hear sounds of Latin, jazz, rock'n'roll, or something else. Best of all, this band plays Japanese American music that most kids like.

Hiroshima started in 1975. There are four main people in the group. Dan Kuramoto is the leader of the band. He plays keyboards and woodwinds, like the shakuhachi. June Kuramoto plays the koto and samisen. Danny Yamamoto is the drummer, and Johnny Mori plays taiko. All four grew up in Los Angeles.

In the past, Hiroshima had a rough time getting recognized. Now it is on its way to becoming a successful band. Hiroshima is selling more albums than ever before and continually wins awards for its music.

This group has many albums. In 1980, they received an award for Breakout Artist of the Year from *Performance Magazine*. "Winds of Change," a song from their second album, was nominated for a Grammy Award. We think it's great that Hiroshima blends old instruments with new ones and comes out with great sounds.

## SINGING

We sang songs every day during our workshop. Some of the names of the songs were "Konnichiwa," "Harugakita," "Sakura," and "Usagi to Kame." We can't put our voices in this book, so if you want to learn these and other songs, you can check out a book and a tape, both called *Japanese Children's Songs* (published by Nihonmachi Little Friends). It is put out by the Japanese American Museum in Los Angeles. These books are available from the Japanese American Curriculum Project (800-874-2242), a nonprofit group that finds resources for teachers. You might also want to buy a tape of Hiroshima. If you're in Florida, stop in and see One World Taiko perform. You might be able to attend some folk dancing or classical dance in your own city.

## DANCING

Besides listening to Japanese American music, we also danced to it. There are two kinds of Japanese dancing: folk dancing and classical dancing. A folk dance is a people's dance. Men, women, and children all dance. You don't have to have a lot of training to do the folk dances. Festivals like Obon (the Festival of Lanterns to honor the dead) are times for folk dancing. Obon is explained earlier in this chapter.

Classical dance takes much longer to learn. Dancers take lessons and practice for many years. The classical dancer performs on a stage and wears lots of make-up and fancier kimonos than folk dancers wear. In both folk dancing and classical dancing, dancers use flowers, fans, hats, scarves, sticks, and *kachi-kachis*. Kachi-kachis are wooden instruments that are clicked between two fingers like castanets.

Each dance has a story to go with it. We learned a dance called *Harugakita* (hah-roo-gah-kee-tah). The parts of this dance tell about the coming of spring in the mountains, plains, and meadows, when the flowers bloom and the birds return. Folk dances follow the same patterns of movements but can be changed by the number of steps. Individual dancers can choreograph classical dances so they can dance them the way they wish. You

*Authors learning a dance for Obon*

Chris Tucker

might see the same dance done differently, depending on who is dancing.

We all learned *Tanko Bushi* (tahn-koh boo-shee), a folk dance about coal mining. This is a circle dance. It is easier to learn a dance from watching someone else dance rather than from reading about it,

*Sensei demonstrating the Tanko Bushi dance*

Chris Tucker

so you might want to ask a Japanese American person in your community to help you. Learning this dance was hard at first. It seemed slow, since it was hard to follow the patterns and stay together in a group. Some people even ran into each other by mistake. But it got easier as we went on. We all wore colorful *happi*, which are kimono coats, and *hachimakis*, which are headbands. In the future, we hope other people will learn the folk dances to carry on the tradition.

## KIMONOS

During special celebrations and festivals, you might see Japanese Americans wearing *kimonos*. Kimono means "the thing worn." Both men and women wear kimonos. The kimono was first worn in Japan during the third or fourth century A.D.

Every kimono has an *obi*, a beautiful sash worn around the chest. The obi is about 15 feet long and 1 foot wide. You can tie an obi in many different ways. You can even show if you are married or not by the way it is tied.

Some people also wear *tabis*, which are like socks; *getas*, which are wooden sandals that are raised up; or *zoris*, which are flat sandals. Undergarments, such as undershirts and half slips, are worn to protect the kimono, which can be very expensive. Hairpieces and handbags are sometimes used as accessories. It can take as long as an hour to get dressed in a kimono.

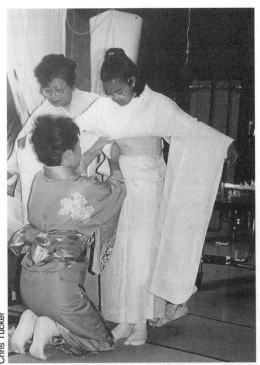

Chris Tucker

*Learning how to tie an obi*

Although many Japanese Americans have kimonos, they wear them only for special festivals like Girls' Day and Obon. Others wear *yukata*, cotton summer kimonos. They also wear kimonos for special occasions like tea ceremonies and folk dances. Kimonos are so beautiful that it's no wonder some are displayed in museums. If you have a chance, attend a Japanese American festival to see these colorful kimonos.

## THE TEA CEREMONY

In the United States, Japanese Americans enjoy drinking tea, but few perform the tea ceremony in their homes. It

was started by Buddhist monks in Japan, who sometimes used the tea for medicine. This tradition is being carried on by some Japanese American cultural organizations. In fact, you might be able to have someone from such an organization come to your school or group to demonstrate the tea ceremony for you. Some Issei and Nisei women came and did a tea ceremony for us.

The tea ceremony is performed in a very special way. It can last from half an hour to an hour and a half, depending on how many people are served. First, a little powdered tea is put into the tea bowl. Then hot water is poured into the bowl, enough for three or four sips. The tea is stirred with a bamboo brush. The tea looks green and foamy and tastes like hot water with a little spice in it.

The server then gives each guest a bowl of tea. The server moves carefully and calmly. Tea ceremonies are never noisy. When the guests drink the tea, they cup their hands around the bowl. There are no handles on

Chris Tucker

*Performing the special tea ceremony*

the bowl, and each tea bowl is different. Part of the pleasure of the tea ceremony comes from the feel of the warm bowl.

Each of us made a tea bowl in art class. It took a lot of concentration. Before we made our pottery, we planned and thought about the style, design, and color. The bowls were a lot of different shapes and sizes. They didn't always turn out the way we wanted, but we thought they looked good anyway. It was really fun to see how the bowls turned out after we glazed and fired them. We wanted to go home and drink some tea from our bowls.

## ARCHITECTURE

In many places across America, you can see examples of Japanese architecture.

Americans have taken Japanese styles and used them in all kinds of buildings, from restaurants to shopping malls.

In many cities throughout the United States, you can find a Japanese American cultural center that is almost like a small town. Some examples of these are the International District (Seattle, Washington), Japan Town (San Francisco, California), Sakura Square (Denver, Colorado), and Little Tokyo (Los Angeles, California). Japanese Americans sponsor festivals and celebrations at these centers, and people of all different heritages come and enjoy them.

If you visit one of these cultural centers, you will see the influence of Japanese architecture in the roofs, gates, doors, and windows. Often you can see a *torii* (toh-

*Japanese styles of architecture can be found all over the U.S.*

Chris Tucker

ree-ee), a wooden gateway with two columns and a crossbar on top. The ends of the crossbar arch upward. In these Japanese American cultural centers, you can find Japanese restaurants, churches, markets, gift shops, travel agencies, and barber shops.

In the restaurants, you might be taken into a room with *tatami* (tah-tah-mee) mats on the floor. These mats are made from rice straw and smell like sweet grass. You take off your shoes before entering this room. You eat at a low table and sit on flat cushions instead of chairs. Some restaurants also have *shoji*, sliding doors, that look like windows with white squares of paper in them. Light can come through, but you can't see through the paper. Keep your eyes open, and you will see many examples of Japanese architecture all across America.

## JAPANESE GARDENS

Japanese gardens are different from the gardens or flowers that many people have in their backyards. The rocks, fountains, and plants used in Japanese gardens in America are not the same as those used in Japan, because our climate is different. Most Japanese Americans do not have a Japanese garden in their backyards, but many other Americans are carrying on this tradition. These gardens are often a blend of Japanese and American styles of landscaping.

If you were to take a tour of special gardens in your city, you might see several that have been influenced by the Japanese style. With the many cultures in our country, it is exciting that Americans of all backgrounds pick up parts of other people's heritages and make them part of their own traditions.

*A Japanese-style garden in Colorado*

Chris Tucker

If you want to see a Japanese garden, go to a botanical garden near your home or visit a Japanese cultural center. Some well-known Japanese gardens are:

- Denver Botanical Gardens in Denver, Colorado
- Japanese Tea Garden in Golden Gate Park, San Francisco, California
- Japanese Garden in the Arboretum in Seattle, Washington
- Japanese Garden in Portland, Oregon
- Japanese Tea Garden in San Mateo, California
- Huntington Library Art Collection in Pasadena, California

- Botanical Garden in San Marino, California
- National Arboretum in Washington, D.C.

## IKEBANA

*Ikebana* (ee-keh-bah-nah) is the art of flower arranging. Although it started in Japan in the 1400s, today some Japanese Americans and other Americans still arrange and display flowers using the traditional techniques and styles. During our workshop, we were given a lesson in ikebana, and we made our own flower

*The art of flower arranging is called ikebana*

Chris Tucker

arrangements. They looked beautiful next to our tea bowls and on the tables for our celebration dinner. We loved the way ikebana made us feel. It can be very relaxing and comforting.

The flowers you use in ikebana depend on the season. Each flower or plant has a special place in the arrangement and means something different. The tallest branches or flowers stand for the heavens. The middle ones stand for the people, and the lowest stand for the earth. It is important to keep the design simple.

There are ten different schools of ikebana but only four basic styles. They are *Rikka*, which is the oldest style; *Morib-*

*ana*, the natural style; *Shoka*, a sleek and delicate style; and *Nageire*, a more casual style.

Ikebana helps us appreciate the beauty and wonder of nature. Though ikebana looks very simple to do, it's not. Creating any of the styles takes a lot of practice and hard work.

Many cities in the U.S. have places that offer ikebana lessons. Japanese festivals in America sometimes have examples of ikebana on display. Many Americans enjoy ikebana as a hobby.

## SUMI-E

*Sumi-e* (soo-mee-eh) is Japanese ink painting. How is sumi-e different from other kinds of painting? One difference is that the artists use ink that they make themselves. To do this they use an inkstone and an ink stick called a *sumi* stick. The sumi stick is made out of carbon from burnt pine.

Before beginning to paint, there are strict rules to follow:

*Japanese calligraphy*

You can find sumi-e paintings in homes, restaurants, and museums. Some Japanese Americans create sumi-e art. If you have a chance, watch someone give a demonstration on sumi-e. You will be amazed at the picture that will appear with just a few strokes of the brush. Sumi-e uses the same brushstrokes as calligraphy.

## CALLIGRAPHY

Calligraphy is the art of fine handwriting. Japanese calligraphy, called *shodo* (shoh-doh), uses the same ink, paper, and brushes that are used for sumi-e painting, which you just read about.

Learning calligraphy is not easy. It takes

- Sit up straight.
- Don't chew gum.
- Put one hand on the paper while you hold the brush with your other hand.
- Get your mind ready to paint.

The basic colors of sumi-e are black and white. Black ink is painted on white paper. Backgrounds are not painted in. The painter considers the white area as the background, and it has special meaning in sumi-e.

When you are first learning sumi-e, you paint simple things, like grass. Then you are ready to paint more difficult objects, like flowers. With just a few brushstrokes, a picture is complete. Each stroke is important to the picture.

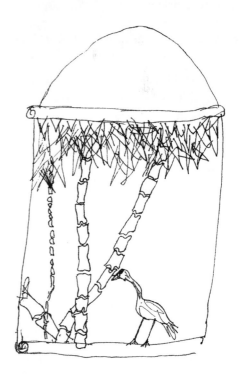

many years to learn the characters in the Japanese language and how to use the calligraphy brush.

If you visit a Japanese American cultural center, you'll see examples of calligraphy.

## JAPANESE AMERICAN ARTISTS

There are many Japanese American artists all across America. We only have room to tell about a few. These artists have blended techniques from their heritage with American ways and developed their own style of artwork. These artists are sort of like pioneers. Read on to see how art became a lifestyle for six famous Japanese American artists.

### Yuzuru Henry Sugimoto (1900–1990)

Yuzuru Sugimoto was a very devoted painter and loved what he did. He did not let anything stop him from painting. In fact, during his time in the internment camps, he painted on bed sheets, fruit packing canvas, and any other material he could find.

Over the years, Mr. Sugimoto did oil paintings of European scenes, designed fabric, and made block prints that showed his Japanese heritage. His work has been displayed in the Smithsonian Institute in Washington D.C., the Wright Art Gallery in Los Angeles, and in the International Gallery in New York.

We enjoyed looking at Mr. Sugimoto's bright and beautiful art work and know he

will not be forgotten. After a long and wonderful life, he died in 1990 at age 90.

### Hisako Hibi (1907–1991)

"Painting knows no color or race," Hisako Hibi once said. "If I want a better house, I can paint one. If I want a road, I can paint a road. And if I want to see beauty, I can see the clouds go by."

Mrs. Hibi loved her grandma, who taught Mrs. Hibi to look for beauty in her life and to work hard. She was married in 1930 and painted lots of things in that decade that were lost when her family was put in the internment camp in 1942. After the war, her pictures changed and became dark and scary. Over the years, they grew lighter, as she remembered what her Grandma had taught her. In fact, her work done in the 1950s was very light and transparent. She explained how her art brought back her memories as colors.

Today you can see her art displayed in galleries across our nation, such as the Japanese American National Museum in Los Angeles.

### Mine Okubo (b. 1912)

Mine Okubo uses painting as a tool to find truth and beauty. Her work is very beautiful and colorful. It is bright and bold. She became famous when she was in her late twenties and did two solo shows in 1940 and 1941.

While in an internment camp, she taught art classes. After the war, she became an illustrator for magazines including *Fortune*, *Life*, and the *Saturday Review*. Her work has changed over the years, from stiff, abstract drawings to still lifes with strong colors and form.

Ms. Okubo has also written a book called *Citizen 13660* that tells about her camp experiences. Ms. Okubo has had many exhibits in the past, including one in the National Museum of Women in the Arts, in Washington, D.C. in 1991.

### Matsumi Mike Kanemitsu (1922–1992)

Matsumi Kanemitsu was born in Ogden, Utah in 1922. He served in the U.S. Army in World War II. After the war, he decided to become an artist. He was an abstract

painter who also made prints using metal plates.

Mr. Kanemitsu's artwork is much different than other abstract painters, because it uses traditional Japanese sumi-e styles and modern American ideas together. This truly expresses the Japanese American heritage. "When a tiger dies, it leaves its fur," he once said. "When a person dies, he leaves his name." We are glad Mr. Kanemitsu left his name on his beautiful and unique art.

### Ruth Asawa (b. 1926)

Ruth Asawa was both unlucky and lucky. She was unlucky because she was put in an internment camp. She was lucky because Tom Okamoto, who had been a Disney artist, taught kids in her camp how to draw and do art. She was born in

1926 in California and put into an internment camp in Rohwer, Arkansas.

After the camp, she studied to be an art teacher at Milwaukee State College. She believes that you can teach children values through art and find the answers to your problems doing art. She has worked with many different kinds of sculptures and has also done graphic arts.

Ruth Asawa has had many exhibits in cities across our nation including New York, Boston, and San Francisco. She has been hired to do many large sculptures and fountains by different cities and companies. Keep your eyes open because someday you might see one of her big sculptures right in front of you.

## MUSEUMS

If you want to learn more about Japanese American culture and art, you might want to visit a museum. Some well-known museums include:

- Bishop Museum in Honolulu, Hawaii
- The Japanese American National Museum in Los Angeles, California
- Morikami (moh-ree-kah-mee) Museum in Del Ray Beach, Florida
- Wing Luke Museum in Seattle, Washington
- The Japanese American Historical Society in San Francisco, California
- Smithsonian National Museum of American History in Washington, D.C.

# FAMOUS FIRSTS AND HEROES

*This chapter is on the brave and bold*
*Men and women, young and old,*
*Who have made our country a better place.*
*They have worked hard for the human race.*

In this chapter, you will find a lot of people who are famous and have been the first to do something. We see them as heroes. These Japanese Americans have been through a lot and have worked hard to overcome problems. Even during bad times, these people have made good things happen. With their courage and determination, they made a difference in many people's lives. Whether you want to be a teacher, a lawyer, a writer, or some other profession, these heroes' stories will inspire you.

In writing this chapter, we found that there aren't a lot of books around that discuss famous Japanese Americans. We decided to write about as many Japanese Americans as possible to try to make sure these people are never forgotten. Some biographies are long, others are short. We did not have the space to include a biography on everyone, so at the end of the chapter, we've also included a list of other famous Japanese Americans. All the biographies are in order by date of birth.

## FEATURED BIOGRAPHIES

### Takino Washimi Takamatsu (1886–1985)

In 1971, Takino Washimi Takamatsu received the Fifth-Class Order of Sacred Treasure from the Japanese government for her efforts in sharing the Japanese culture. She was the first woman in Colorado to receive the medal, which is given to naturalized American citizens from Japan. She taught people how to play the koto, do *ikebana* (flower arranging), and perform the tea ceremony until she was in her

Chris Tucker

*These are kotos, the instrument that Takino Takamatsu taught people how to play*

nineties. Mrs. Takamatsu died December 29, 1985, at the age of 99.

Mrs. Takamatsu was born on April 24, 1886, at the Kokutaiji Temple in Hiroshima, Japan. Her father was a Zen priest descended from samurai warriors. Mrs. Takamatsu got a good education when she was a child. Her father died when she was only seven, so Mrs. Takamatsu and her mother moved from the temple. Unfortunately, the person handling her father's will stole their money. When she grew older, Mrs. Takamatsu became a teacher so she could support her mom and herself.

Years later, Mrs. Takamatsu met Saburo Takamatsu. They got married and left for California where Mr. Takamatsu had already started a peach orchard and a strawberry farm. Then Mr. Takamatsu died of lung cancer. After her husband's death, Mrs. Takamatsu continued to teach in Colusa, California, and raise her four children. When World War II began, the Japanese School closed and the government ordered a curfew. When Executive Order 9066 was posted on a telephone pole on their block, it instructed the Japanese Issei and Nissei to leave the area within a week.

Home in the internment camp meant one room in a wooden barrack with brick floors. The only source of heat during the cold winter days was a potbellied stove. Mrs. Takamatsu was ordered not to teach the Japanese language, so she taught knitting instead. At the end of World War II, Mrs. Takamatsu left for Denver. There she found work re-weaving Oriental rugs at Sarkisian's Oriental Rug Shop. She worked there until she was in her eighties. She kept on teaching at the Japanese Language School at the Denver Buddhist Temple into her nineties.

### John Aiso (1909–1987)

Imagine you want to be the student body president or a leader in your neighborhood, but all the people who want the same thing are different from you. You might feel scared, or you might stand up for yourself and make them see that you are just as smart as everyone else. Well, that is what John Aiso did.

Mr. Aiso was born in Los Angeles in 1909. He started standing up for himself at age

Courtesy of Archie A. Miyatake

*John Aiso*

13. He went to Hollywood High School and decided he wanted to be student body president. Lots of people in the school thought he was very smart and voted for him. After he won, many parents in the school said he wasn't a real American because he was of Japanese American heritage. In response, the principal canceled all student government activities until Mr. Aiso graduated. He felt that if Mr. Aiso couldn't be president, no one could.

After graduating from Hollywood High School, Mr. Aiso studied for one year in Tokyo, Japan. At age 17, he entered Brown University. He graduated from the school with good grades and was chosen to speak at graduation because of his academic ability. He later attended Harvard Law

School and joined a New York law firm after graduation. In 1939, Mr. Aiso went back to Los Angeles. During World War II, he was the chief instructor at the Military Intelligence Language School, retiring from there as a colonel. Earl Warren, who was then the governor of California, appointed Mr. Aiso to be municipal court judge in Los Angeles in 1953. He was the first Japanese American to be a superior court judge on the mainland.

Sadly, Mr. Aiso was killed by a mugger at a gas station in 1987.

### Tsuyako "Sox" Kitashima (b. 1918)

You can't erase negative events of the past, but you can keep them from happening again. This is what Ms. Tsuyako Kitashima tells others. Better known as "Sox" Kitashima, she is a civil rights activist. That means she stands up for the rights of her people. In fact, Ms. Kitashima has stood up not only for her rights as a Japanese American, but also for the rights of other people as well.

Ms. Kitashima began her fight for civil rights in 1979. She spoke to the members of Congress who were holding hearings about Japanese Americans held in internment camps during World War II.

From 1979 to 1989, many Japanese American groups worked hard to pass a bill called the American Civil Liberties Act, to help people understand how unfair it was to put Japanese Americans in the camps. Ms. Kitashima worked very hard on this bill. She collected more than 25,000 letters to take to Washington, D.C. She also tried to

*Tsuyako "Sox" Kitashima (second from left) with friends at the Department of Justice*

talk to as many people as she could in Congress to get the bill passed. After three tries, it finally passed in 1988.

### Yoshiko Uchida (b. 1921)

How would you like it if many guards were always watching you, making sure you didn't do anything wrong? Would you write about it? Well, Yoshiko Uchida did. She wrote about her experiences in a World War II internment camp.

Ms. Uchida, a Nisei, is the first Japanese American to write full-time for young readers. Her books help students and even adults understand what it was like living in Topaz, an internment camp in Utah. She named her first book *Journey to Topaz* (New York: Charles Scribner, 1971).

Yoshiko Uchida was born in Alameda, California, and grew up in the 1930s. In 1942, she and her family were put in an internment camp. Ms. Uchida saw many sad things there. There was not enough food, and some people died because of this. Around this time, she wrote her first book on brown wrapping paper.

One of the helpful things Ms. Uchida did in the camp was to volunteer to teach school, so that children could keep learning. The whole time Ms. Uchida was in Topaz, she kept a journal about the sad and happy moments of her life.

When Ms. Uchida grew older, she decided that she wanted to write stories about being Japanese American. She has written many books for young readers about Japan and Japanese American children in the United States. She wants them to understand and appreciate their heritage. She also wants all children to know that everyone should be treated the same no matter what.

## Judge Lance Ito

"Guilty or "not guilty"—what do you think of when you hear those words? We think of court. You may have seen Judge Lance Ito in court on television. He was the judge for the O.J. Simpson trial in Los Angeles, California. But there is more to Judge Ito than what you may have seen on television.

Mr. Ito is a Japanese American judge. He was born in the Silver Lake area in Los Angeles. Both of his parents were schoolteachers who met while interned in a Japanese relocation camp during World War II. They lost everything when they were put into the camps, and it was hard for them to start over again. Mr. Ito knew about his parents having to go to the camps. He never brought up this awful subject but says that his parents' experiences affect him in everything he does. Mr. Ito feels that since his parents were denied a fair chance, he is inspired to do whatever he can to make sure that others are always treated fairly.

As a boy, Mr. Ito grew up like many other American children. He went fishing with his father and still loves to fish, even though he doesn't have a lot of time for it now. He always thought he was a good fisherman, until he took his wife on her first fishing trip. His wife, Margaret York, caught the first fish, the last fish, the biggest fish, and the most fish. Mr. Ito thinks that fly fishing is a very difficult art, but his wife feels there is nothing to it.

One of Mr. Ito's role models growing up was Delbert Wong. Along with being young Lance's Boy Scoutmaster, Delbert Wong was one of the first Asian judges in the continental United States. Mr. Wong may have been one of the reasons that Mr. Ito got into the field of law. Even today, the two judges remain good friends.

After graduating from Boalt Hall Law School at the University of California at Berkeley, Mr. Ito went into private law practice and worked in the Los Angeles County District Attorney's office. He was appointed to be a judge in 1987. In 1992, Mr. Ito was honored as the "Trial Judge of the Year" by the Los Angeles Bar Association.

Mr. Ito believes that we need rules to run a country and that we must always practice fairness. He tries to find the truth in any way possible, because he knows that sometimes innocent people get charged with crimes they didn't commit. To make sure this doesn't happen, Mr. Ito spends as much time needed for the truth to come out. He says that the two things that a judge needs are patience and knowing when to keep your mouth shut.

One of Mr. Ito's goals for the future is to work inside the juvenile court system. He hopes that he can change the way that troubled kids think before they grow up. Mr. Ito said that when people are fully grown, their minds cannot be changed easily. Therefore, it's difficult for them to change and to stay away from a life of crime. Mr. Ito feels that by getting involved in the juvenile court system, he can mold troubled kids into citizens who can contribute to society.

We think that Mr. Lance Ito is an extraordinary man and judge. We hope that he continues to be a judge, because he is a great one. His parents should be proud.

## Ellison S. Onizuka (1946–1986)

Lots of kids hope that one day they might fly in a rocket to the moon or travel to the stars, like they do in *Star Trek*. Going up in space was also a dream for Ellison S. Onizuka, the first Japanese American astronaut.

Mr. Onizuka's sisters remember him as a rascal when he was young. He liked to take things apart around the house. One New Year's Eve, he found an unlit firecracker called a "roman candle," and took it to the basement to see how it worked. He had seen adults light this type of firecracker before, so he lit it himself. Upstairs, his family heard loud thumps through the floor as the candle smoked and exploded. Panicking, his family ran downstairs and found him testing his first rocket. As Mr. Onizuka grew up, he wanted more and more to be an astronaut.

Courtesy of *Tozai Times*

*Lt. Col. Ellison Onizuka*

Mr. Onizuka was born on June 24, 1946. He had two older sisters and one younger brother. Since Mr. Onizuka was the first-born son, he was treated differently from his brother and sisters. He had more chores to do than his brother, and he had to work in his father's store and in the coffee fields. Young Onizuka had a good imagination. In fact, it was so good that he would take his brother for rides in a cardboard box that he pretended was a car.

Mr. Onizuka attended elementary and high schools in Hawaii, later attending the University of Colorado. He was stationed at Vance Air Force base in Oklahoma for his astronaut training, which started in 1978.

The first space flight that Mr. Onizuka went on was the Discovery flight. There were five men on board on January 24,

1985. He felt sad because he could not tell his friends about the flight because it was top secret. After the flight, someone had asked him how high he had been above the earth, but he couldn't even reveal that. "Next question," he had told his friend. That's how top secret it was.

On January 28, 1986, Ellison Onizuka went on another very important space flight. The control room started the countdown. Ten . . . 9 . . . 8 . . . 7 . . . 6 . . . 5 . . . 4 . . . 3 . . . 2 . . . 1 . . . 0. . . . Blast off! Only seconds after its takeoff, something went wrong in the engines and the *Challenger* exploded, killing all seven astronauts inside. We think that Mr. Onizuka was a brave man for going on the *Challenger* shuttle, and we are sad that he died at such a young age. Mr. Onizuka was very close to many people who will remember him. In fact, Americans

will always remember Mr. Ellison Onizuka and the *Challenger* tragedy of 1986.

### Kristi Yamaguchi (b. 1971)

"When I'm skating, I feel like I can express myself," says Kristi Yamaguchi, the first Japanese American woman ever to win an Olympic gold medal for ice skating. "I feel free."

Kristi Tsuya Yamaguchi was born on July 12, 1971, in Hayward, California, growing up in Fremont, near San Francisco. Some people don't know that she was born and raised in California. They think she is from Japan. In fact, she hardly speaks any Japanese at all. Her father is a dentist, and her mother is a medical secretary. Both of her parents spent time in the internment

*Kristi Yamaguchi*

Tana J. Monji

camps during World War II. Kristi is a fourth-generation Japanese American, or Yonsei.

When Kristi was born, she had club feet. The term "club feet" comes from the club-like look of the feet—an inward and downward turning of each foot. For many years as a child, she had to wear corrective shoes to straighten her feet out.At age five, she started taking skating lessons. She was eight years old when she entered her first competition. The next year, she got up at 4:00 a.m. every day so that she could skate for several hours before school. She did this because she was determined to win competitions.

In 1985, she was paired with Rudi Galindo, another skater. They won fifth place at the National Junior Championships. In 1989, Kristi won two medals—a gold medal in pairs competition and a second place in the singles competition at the National Championships. At the World Championships in Paris, she was rated the sixth-best singles skater in the world.

Kristi was 20 years old when she won a gold medal in figure skating for the United States at the 1992 Winter Olympics. After she received this medal, she won her second World Championship, becoming the first female skater to successfully defend her world title since Ms. Peggy Fleming did it in 1968.

Besides skating, Kristi likes to play tennis, go rollerblading, read, dance, and cheer for the San Francisco 49ers football team. She attends the Alameda Buddhist Temple. She is popular wherever she goes. Because she is so famous, she has become a hero to many kids, and adults, too. She has been honored by the San Francisco Asian Chamber of Commerce, a national business-women's association, the Pan Asian National Chamber of Commerce, and the Japanese American Citizens League.

## SHORT BIOGRAPHIES

### Joseph Heco (1837–1897)

Hikozo Hamada, later known as Joseph Heco, was only 13 years old when he got lost in a big storm on the sea. For 50 days, his boat drifted toward America.

An American ship rescued Mr. Hamada and the other sailors, and took them to the United States. Mr. Hamada met a lot of people here. One of them was the president of the United States, Abraham Lincoln.

Mr. Hamada became a citizen of the United States in 1858 and changed his name to Joseph Heco. He was the first Japanese person to become an American citizen, almost 100 years before any other Japanese were allowed to become citizens.

Many years later, he returned to Japan to work for the United States and Japanese governments as an interpreter.

### Fred Wada (b. 1908)

Have you ever dreamed of being a millionaire? Fred Wada did—and became one himself. Mr. Wada was born in Cali-

*Fred Wada with his wife in a Nisei parade*

fornia in 1908. He is famous for advising and working for the Olympic committee.

When he was young, Mr. Wada went to Japan to live with his grandparents. He returned to the United States when he was nine. At age 12, he had to leave home to make room for his younger brothers and sisters. When he was 15, he quit school and got a job delivering milk. When he had saved enough money, Mr. Wada started his own fruit stand, which later became a chain of produce stores across America.

In 1959, Mr. Wada got a letter from Japan asking him to help get votes from other countries, so that the Olympic Games could be held in Japan. He made a deal with Mexico that if Japan could host the 1964 Olympics, he would help Mexico host the

1968 Olympics. The deal worked, and both countries got what they wanted. The 1964 Olympics were held in Tokyo, and the 1968 Olympics were held in Mexico City.

Mr. Wada was an adviser to Mexico and Japan for several years. Later he became interested in fundraising for a nursing home. Mr. Wada gave $1 million to charity. He has donated large amounts of money to the poor.

Mr. Wada is a perfect example of a self-made man—someone who did things on his own.

### John Naka (b. 1914)

Have you ever seen the miniature Japanese trees called bonsai? You may have wondered how they are shaped or who makes

*Bonsai tree*

them. John Naka teaches the art of bonsai throughout the United States, India, Japan, and other countries. Mr. Naka has devoted his life to keeping the art of bonsai alive.

Mr. Naka was born in Colorado and studied bonsai in Japan. At age 21, he moved back to Colorado and started farming in Brighton. He later married Alice Mizunaga and moved to Los Angeles to teach the art of bonsai.

A display of Mr. Naka's trees is in the United States National Arboretum in Washington, D.C. (An arboretum is like a big garden that people can look at or visit.) Mr. Naka is so famous for the art of bonsai that he is often called "Mr. Bonsai."

## Mike Masaoka (1915–1991)

Mike Masaoka never gave up on fighting for Japanese Americans' civil rights—the rights guaranteed to all citizens of the United States. These include speaking and living freely.

Mr. Masaoka was born on October 15, 1915, in Fresno, California. When he was a year old, his family moved to Salt Lake City and opened a grocery store. His father died when Mr. Masaoka was nine. As he grew older, he wanted people to know how much he loved America. He wanted them to know that although he looked Japanese, he was an American.

He joined the Japanese American Citizens League (JACL). Members of the JACL went around the country telling everybody that Japanese Americans were just like other people. Japanese Americans play, sing, and eat just like anybody else.

Courtesy of *Tozai Times*

*Mike Masaoka*

He helped convince the U.S. government to let Japanese Americans serve in the U.S. armed forces, and he was the first to join after the country changed its policy in 1943.

Despite his work for his country, Mr. Masaoka's family was sent to Manzanar Internment Camp while he fought for the United States in Europe.

## Sadao Munemori (1923–1945)

Sadao Munemori was the first Nisei to get a Congressional Medal of Honor as a hero in World War II. This medal is the highest honor given by the U.S. military.

Mr. Munemori was born in 1923. He joined the army after finishing high school. He asked to be moved to a combat unit

Later, Mrs. Harami transferred to work in another area of research at JPL. She says she did her most important work at this time, studying chromosomes.

Mrs. Harami, a Nisei, was born in 1925 in Long Beach, California. Still living in California, she is retired and enjoys raising her dogs and traveling around the country to show them. Mrs. Harami has proven to us that women can do anything they want if they're determined.

and joined the 442nd Regimental Combat Team, a troop made up of Japanese Americans. On April 5, 1945, he died after diving on a grenade to save the lives of two other American soldiers. He was 22 years old. His family was given a Medal of Honor in his memory.

### Sayuri Harami (b. 1925)

Sayuri Harami was one of the first Japanese American women to be hired by the California Institute of Technology's Jet Propulsion Laboratory (JPL). JPL is the center for unmanned space science.

When Mrs. Harami worked on the space program, she worked with computers for the Ranger, Surveyor, Mariner, and Viking space projects. These were the names of spacecraft sent to study the surfaces of Mercury, Venus, Mars, and the moon.

### Patsy Takemoto Mink (b. 1927)

Patsy Takemoto Mink is a very important woman in Hawaii. She was the first female Japanese American lawyer in Hawaii. She is also the first Nisei woman to be elected to the U.S. House of Representatives.

Ms. Mink was born on the island of Maui and lived most of her life in Hawaii. She got her law degree from the University of Chicago in 1951, working very hard in election campaigns during the 1950s. It was an exciting day in 1964 when Ms. Mink was elected to the House of Representatives. She fought for childcare laws, for nondiscrimination, and for women to be recognized for their accomplishments.

### Dr. Paul I. Terasaki (b. 1929)

Everyone was in shock after the 1986 partial meltdown of the Chernobyl nuclear reactor in the former Soviet Union. After the accident, Paul I. Terasaki traveled to Russia to help the people who were suffering from radiation sickness. Radiation sickness is caused by nuclear radiation. The doctors who rushed to Chernobyl risked their lives to assist the sick people. Some of the procedures they used to help people wouldn't have been available if it hadn't been for Dr.

*Dr. Paul Terasaki*

Terasaki. He and the people who worked with him discovered the art of "tissue-typing"—a procedure vital for organ transplants.

Dr. Terasaki is a doctor in Los Angeles. He's a scientist in the medical field of matching blood types. He works to make certain you get the right blood when you need it. His job is important, because if you get the wrong blood type, you could get very sick.

Dr. Terasaki is the winner of many awards, such as the Netherlands Red Cross Medal, the Modern Medicine Award for Distinguished Achievement, UCLA's Distinguished Achievement Award, and the American Society of Clinical Pathologists-Philip Levine Award. He cares for people all around the world. He displayed this caring when he helped the people of Chernobyl.

### Edison Uno (1929–1976)

Edison Uno was a fighter for justice. His lifelong goal was to make the U.S. government admit that it had made a mistake when it put Japanese Americans in internment camps during World War II.

Mr. Uno was born on October 19, 1929. In 1942, his father was arrested and his family was ordered to go to living quarters at the Santa Anita Race Track in California. After the war, Mr. Uno returned to live in California. There he finished his education and married Rosalind Kido.

In 1972, the U.S. government removed Title II of the McCarran International Security Act of 1950. This act said you could put people in jail without a trial if they were suspected spies. Mr. Uno worked hard to overturn this act, because he felt it was unconstitutional.

On December 24, 1976, Mr. Uno had a heart attack and died. It seemed that all of his work for the government's apology to the Japanese Americans had been in vain. Then, in 1984, the U.S. government formally apologized for its mistake in sending the Japanese Americans to internment camps during World War II.

### Norman Mineta (b. 1931)

Have you ever dreamed of being an elected leader of your city? In 1971, Norman Mineta was elected mayor of San Jose, California.

*Norman Mineta (center) with supporters*

Later, he became the first Japanese American member of Congress from the continental United States.

Mr. Mineta was born in San Jose on November 12, 1931. When he was a child, he and his family were forced out of their home and sent to an internment camp.

When he got out of the internment camp, he got his high school diploma and went to college. He earned a Bachelor of Science degree in business at the University of California at Berkeley in 1953. After that, Mr. Mineta went on duty for the U.S. Army as an intelligence officer.

When he got out of the army, Mr. Mineta got involved in community activities. In 1962, he joined the San Jose Human Relations Commission, his first public post. Mr. Mineta also became a member of the San Jose City Council in 1967.

### Noriyuki "Pat" Morita (b. 1932)

Many people dream of one day becoming a famous actor. After years of hard work as a computer operator, disc jockey, actor, and comedian, Noriyuki Morita became a big hit in the movie *The Karate Kid*. Kids all over began to say lines from the movie. Since then, he has been in many other popular films.

Mr. Morita was born in 1932 in Iselton, California. During his childhood, he overcame a spinal disease and living in an internment camp. These things taught him to be brave and to not give up.

*Noriyuki "Pat" Morita in* The Karate Kid

As an actor, Mr. Morita was nominated for an Academy Award in 1985 for *The Karate Kid*, receiving the Lifetime Achievement Award from the Association of Asian/Pacific American Artists in 1987. He also acted on *Happy Days*, an old television show.

## Lawson Fusao Inada (b. 1938)

"Writing can be fun," says Lawson Fusao Inada, the co-owner of Kids Matter, a publishing company for children. His company is a place where kids can learn to become novelists, poets, or any kind of writer they choose.

Mr. Inada wrote the first book of poetry by an Asian American to be published by a large company. Mr. Inada's most famous work, *Before the War*, was published in 1971 (New York: William Morrow). He has also written many other books that have been published by more than ten companies.

Mr. Inada was one of 21 American writers chosen to read his poetry at the White House. He taught classes in six states about different backgrounds and ways of learning. Mr. Inada has read and spoken at major colleges all over the U.S.

In 1984, he received an award for excellence in teaching from the Oregon State Board of Higher Education. In 1985, Mr. Inada served as the U.S. representative to the World Cultural Festival in Berlin, Germany. He has lectured throughout that country. Mr. Inada is currently serving on the Commission on Racism and Bias in Education.

## Daniel Nakamura (b. 1957)

Do you like to fold things? Daniel Nakamura is the king of origami—the art of Japanese paper folding. He is famous for his amazing creations of paper cranes, life-sized penguins, and enormous roses. He learned his origami skill from his grandma.

Mr. Nakamura was born in 1957. His family is also very artistic. His brother is a well-known illustrator who teaches at the Art Center College of Design. His uncle is the designer of some of the early Corvette automobiles.

Mr. Nakamura once had to make a paper crane 19 feet by 18 feet. That's big! The paper he worked with is larger than the carpet in our bedrooms! He doesn't only do origami for a living. He also makes

Courtesy of Tozai Times

*Daniel Nakamura, the king of origami*

sculptures, paints with watercolors, and teaches at Venice High School in California.

We did origami in our workshop, and we thought it was fun. Try it for yourself.

## MORE FAMOUS FIRSTS AND HEROES

Here are some more people you may want to learn about. There is a recent encyclopedia about famous Japanese Americans. It's called *An A to Z Japanese American History: Reference from 1868 to the Present* (New York: Facts on File, 1993). This might be a good place for you to look for more stuff.

**Mitsuye Endo**  (b. 1920)
Won the first favorable court decision for the Nisei about the internment camps.

**Warren Furutani**  (b. 1947)
First Japanese American to be president of the Los Angeles city school board.

**Samuel Hayakawa**  (1906–1992)
Served as a U.S. senator from California between 1977 and 1983. Also became known as an educator.

**John Kiyoshi Hirasaki**  (b. 1941)
NASA manned spacecraft scientist.

**Lorie Hirose**  (b. 1961)
Won an Emmy Award in 1991 for her work on a documentary. Works as a reporter for 9-KUSA News in Denver, Colorado.

**William Hosokawa**  (b. 1915)
First foreign correspondent for the *Denver Post*. Wrote *Nisei: The Quiet Americans* in 1969.

**Mamoru Iga**  (b. 1916)
Author of *The Thorn in the Chyrsanthemum: Suicide and Economic Success in Modern Japan.*

**Daniel K. Inouye**  (b. 1924)
First Japanese American elected to U.S. Senate (represents Hawaii). Fought in WWII and earned a Distinguished Service Cross.

*Sen. Daniel K. Inouye*

**Tomi Kanazawa**
First Nisei to appear in a leading role with the Metropolitan Opera Company.

**Saburo Kido**  (1902-1977)
Founded the Japanese American
Citizens League in 1930.

**Jin Kinoshita**  (b. 1922)
An ophthalmologist who pioneered
research on "sugar" cataracts.

**Ann Kiyomura**  (b. 1955)
Won Wimbledon women's doubles
title in 1975.

**Tommy Kono**  (b. 1930)
Won Olympic weightlifting titles for
the U.S. in 1952 and 1956, and a silver
medal in 1960.

**Ben Kuroki**  (b. 1918)
Won the Air Force Distinguished Flying
Cross as a gunner on a bomber in WWII.

Sirlin Photographers

*Doris Matsui*

**William Marutani**  (b. 1923)
First Japanese American lawyer to
argue and win a case before the
National Supreme Court.

**Doris Matsui**  (b. 1944)
Appointed to President Clinton's
cabinet as Deputy Director of Public
Liaison for the President.

**Robert Matsui**  (b. 1941)
Elected to represent California in the
U.S. House of Representatives in 1979.

**George Matsumoto**  (b. 1922)
Recipient of numerous awards in
architecture.

**Shigemi Matsumoto**
Rising opera singer and the only
Japanese American member of the
San Francisco Opera Company.

**Masayuki Matsunaga**  (1916-1990)
Served as a U.S. Representative and
Senator from Hawaii and was also a
decorated war hero.

**Cynthia Mayeda**  (b. 1949)
Leader in the field of business and
charitable organizations.

**Frank Shotaro Miyamoto**  (b. 1912)
Sociologist at the University of
Washington.

**Hiroshi "Hershey" Miyamoto** (b. 1926)
Awarded the Congressional Medal of Honor.

**Kent Nagano**   (b. 1951)
International conductor currently with the Berkeley Symphony.

**Isamu Noguchi**   (1904–1988)
Noted sculptor, best known for the relief sculpture he created for the Associated Press building in Rockefeller Center in New York. He was also a consultant for the design of John F. Kennedy's tomb.

**Sono Osato**   (b. 1919)
Dancer with the famous Ballet Russe.

**James Sakamoto**   (1903–1955)
First Nisei boxer to fight professionally at Madison Square Garden. Also published the first Japanese American newspaper in English.

**Makoto Sakamoto**   (b. 1947)
Led the U.S. men's gymnastics squad in the Tokyo Olympics in 1964.

**Eric Sato**   (b. 1966)
Played on the 1992 U.S. Olympic men's volleyball team with his brother, Gary.

**Gary Sato**   (b. 1955)
Played on the 1992 U.S. Olympic men's volleyball team with his brother, Eric.

**Liana Sato**   (b. 1964)
Played on the 1992 U.S. Olympic women's volleyball team. Eric and Gary Sato are her brothers.

**Kosaku Sawada**
Developed new varieties of the camellia shrub.

**Suma Sugi**   (b. 1906)
In 1930, became the first Nisei lobbyist.

**Pat Suzuki**   (b. 1931)
Recording star and actress. Her outstanding role was the lead in *The Flower Drum Song*.

**Joseph Swensen**   (b. 1960)
Famous violinist and graduate of Juilliard School of Music.

**Shinkichi Tajiri**   (b. 1923)
Famous sculptor of bronze and brass. Has received many honors and awards.

**Irene Takahashi**
Lawyer and municipal court judge in California.

**Jokichi Takamine**   (1854–1922)
A chemist who was the first to isolate pure adrenaline. He founded the Nippon Club in New York to improve understanding of U.S. and Japanese relations.

**Tritia Toyota**
One of the first Japanese American news anchors on television. She works in the Los Angeles area.

**Miyoshi Umeki** (b. 1929)
Won an Academy Award as Best Supporting Actress in 1957 for the movie *Sayonara*.

**Newton (Uyesugi) Wesley**
An optometrist whose work played a large part in perfecting plastic contact lenses.

**Rev. Seigen Haruo Yamaoka** (b. 1934)
First Nisei to be Bishop of the Buddhist Church of America in San Francisco.

**Thomas Yatabe** (b. 1897)
First Nisei licensed to practice dentistry in California. First national president of the Japanese American Citizens League.

**Karl Yoneda** (b. 1906)
Author of *History of Japanese Labor in the United States*.

**Hideki Yukawa** (1907–1981)
Received the Nobel Prize for Physics.

# KIDS WHO MAKE A DIFFERENCE

*Heroes come from big to small.*
*They are those who help us all.*
*In this chapter, you will find*
*People who are young and kind.*

In this chapter, you will learn about some of the young Japanese Americans who have contributed a lot to make their communities better. Some of these young heroes have also tried to help other communities by aiding people who live in these places. Others have made or done something to help people understand the Japanese American culture.

The young people featured in this chapter have made an impact on society. We hope you will admire them and learn about the things that they have done.

## Emily Imatani

Twenty-one-year-old Emily Imatani thinks of herself not as a hero, but as a regular person who wants to help others. Emily went to Mississippi over her spring break from the University of Colorado-Boulder.

However, she didn't go for a vacation. She went to help the community there. She

*Emily Imatani*

teamed up with Habitat for Humanity and helped build a house for those less fortunate than she.

Emily and some of her friends piled into a van and drove for 16 hours straight to Coahoma, Mississippi. When they got there, instead of staying in a fancy hotel, they stayed in an abandoned schoolhouse. They slept on bunk beds in their own sleeping bags and cooked their own food. This doesn't sound very comfortable, but Emily said it was fun.

She and the other workers woke up at 7:00 a.m. to start working on the house. She said it wasn't hard work, but we figured it was. While she was in Mississippi, Emily went to visit a school where many children hadn't seen a Japanese American woman in person. Some of the kids asked to touch her hair. Most of the children were African

American. They said they hadn't seen or felt hair so soft.

This year, Emily is a senior in college. Someday she would like to become a criminal lawyer. This summer, she is taking a class to get ready for a test to go to law school. Although working with Habitat for Humanity is a great accomplishment, it is not the only thing Emily can be proud of. She is using her spare time to go to the Boulder District Attorney's office and help crime victims over the phone. She takes calls from people who need help or have questions about the law.

When she was a little girl, Emily liked to go to her father's office, where he worked as an attorney. She remembers wanting to be a designer, artist, or athlete in the Olympics when she grew up. Besides her dad, Emily has her mother, Peggy, her sister, Claire, and three dogs in her family. They all live in Littleton, Colorado. Emily says her family has given her a lot of support and always taught her to do her best.

In the future, Emily wants to be a happy, healthy, and productive person. She wants kids to know that it isn't difficult to get involved with helping people the way she has. She hopes more people will care about others, because the world would be a better place if they did. We think Emily should be proud of how she takes action to show she cares.

### Drew Domoto

Guess who won a trip to the 1994 Winter Olympics in Lillehammer, Norway? One

*Drew Domoto*

of the authors of this book did—Drew Domoto.

Drew is 16 years old. His birthday is October 1, 1979. He has three other people in his family: Nancy, his mother; Milt, his father; and Dara, his 13-year-old sister.

Three years ago, Drew was in his art class, when his teacher, Mrs. Luther, told him about a drawing contest sponsored by VISA and the *Denver Post*. The drawing needed to show what kids thought the Olympics would look like in 100 years—the year 2094. The prize for the winning drawing was a free trip to the 1994 Winter Olympics in Norway. Children from all around the United States entered the art competition. Drew knew there could be only one winner picked from the Rocky Mountain states. He decided to give it a try anyway.

Drew got many of his ideas for his drawing from science-fiction movies and books. Every day for three weeks, he worked on the picture in his art classes. He even took it home to work on it there, too. Finally, after three tries, he felt he could turn in his drawing.

Drew didn't hear anything for weeks, so he figured he didn't win. Then he got a phone call. It was a woman from the *Denver Post*. She said Drew was the Rocky Mountain winner and that he would be one of the ten artists to go to Norway from the U.S.A. When he heard that he had won, Drew was so happy that he screamed his brains out and jumped up and down.

Finally, the day of his big trip arrived. Drew and his mom got on a plane for New York City, where they met the other U.S. winners and the five Canadian winners. Even though Drew was the only Japanese American in the group, he met and traveled with kids of Jewish, Chinese, Hispanic, and Norwegian heritage. Everyone got along no matter where they were from.

Drew's adventures really began when he arrived in Norway. The Americans and Canadians met the ten Norwegian winners, and they all got to be in the opening ceremonies of the Winter Olympics. They also saw some of the other events. In between, Drew appeared on TV and did newspaper and radio interviews.

*Drew's winning drawing*

Drew traded pins with other kids while he was in Norway. He met people from all over the world this way. A lot of them thought he was from Japan at first. They were a little surprised when he said he was a Japanese American.

The young artists also got to see what Norway's culture was like when they ate reindeer, rabbit, pickled herring, and a delicious brown goat cheese. Drew was surprised that Norwegians ate so much fish. One of the dishes they eat is a fish cake that tasted very much like the kamaboko Drew eats at home. What a great experience! We're sure it's a trip he'll never forget.

Drew likes to do other things, too. He is a black belt in karate, a co-captain of his freshman basketball team, a member of his high school track team, and a member of the Japanese Club. He is now taking a Japanese language class in school. This year, one of Drew's artworks was selected to hang in the Colorado State Capitol with 100 other works from kids all over the state. Drew is also proud to be one of the authors of this book you're reading now. You can see some of his illustrations on other pages.

We think Drew's pictures have made a difference in his own life and in the lives of others. We hope he keeps up all his excellent work!

## Kimiko Roberts

Kimiko Elaine Leola Jenica Roberts is her full name. Kimiko has many names from her many different cultural backgrounds. She was born on February 7, 1976. Her dad is African American. He has a little Native American and Mexican heritage, too. Her mom is a Sansei, or third generation Japanese American. This makes Kimiko a Yonsei, or fourth generation. She has two sisters, ages 13 and 8, and a brother who is 22.

Kimiko grew up in a Latino neighborhood in east Los Angeles, California. She told us she had the best times as a child at family activities like barbecues and vacations. Her family celebrated holidays such as Christmas, Easter, and the Japanese New Year with lots of Japanese foods.

*Kimiko Roberts (bottom left) and her family*

Kimiko has many good memories, but she remembers some bad experiences, too. When she was little, some kids teased her because she looked different than them. Kimiko tried to remember that she was special. Her mother, father, and *Ba-chan* (grandmother) helped her be proud of who she is. She told us that her mom is her hero.

Being teased about being multiracial encouraged Kimiko to make a video about her culture. Kimiko went to school in Northridge, California, and one summer when she was 13 years old, she saw an ad for a summer video class. Kimiko always kept a journal of her feelings of being multiracial, so she used her journal to make a video showing misunderstandings about Asian American girls. When she was 15, she made another video about herself and the many cultures she represents. Many people who have seen her videos have come to a better understanding of multiracial people.

Now her goal is to make another video.

She wants to show people that kids who are multiracial often go through an identity crisis like she did. This includes problems such as not knowing what race to pick on application forms. She also told us that as she gets older, other issues come up, such as dating and affirmative action. She wants to talk about these and other issues in her next video.

We wanted to know more about Kimiko, so we asked her what she's wanted to be growing up. She told us that at first she wanted to be a fashion designer, but later she wanted to be an architect. She has studied Japanese classical dancing for ten years and has a professional degree in dancing. Right now, she goes to college at the University of California at Berkeley. She's a sophomore and looking for a career in communications after college.

Kimiko told us that if she could change one thing in our country, she would change the way children are educated. "If we don't respect children or the people who teach them," she said, "then we can't make changes." She would like to work with educational and public television when she graduates, in order to help change education. She encouraged us to keep seeking more education because it helps people develop themselves.

These are some of the things we heard in Kimiko's videos:

"No, I do not answer to China Doll, Geisha Girl, Suzie Wong, Mama-san, Jap, or Chink."

"Our histories will be told loudly. We are not invisible."

"Asian America will go on and on, 'cause Asian America is in the heart."

Kimiko also shared these thoughts with us: "I'd like up-and-coming generations of Japanese Americans to examine their culture. They will discover the beauty and elegance that embodies who and what they are."

Kimiko is helping people learn about others. We hope she makes lots more videos in the future.

## Michi Imamura

"And the winner of the YMCA Volunteer of the Year Award is Michi Imamura!" announced the speaker at the awards ceremony. "Congratulations for a job well done." This was one of the most exciting things that happened to Michi Imamura, another young Japanese American who is making a difference. Seventeen-year-old Michi Imamura is very active in the YMCA, and he's volunteered for many activities, mostly involving young children and their summer camps.

Michi's parents are Debbie and Ryo Imamura. Ryo is a college professor and Buddhist priest (see his profile in the Real People chapter), and Debbie is the business manager for the local YMCA. Michi has a little brother named Kaya. He says that his parents taught him some important values. They often told him to have an optimistic outlook on life and to believe that he could make a difference.

Michi always wanted to get involved with his community. When he and his family moved to Olympia, Washington, his mother

*Michi Imamura*

got a job at the local YMCA. After getting involved in basketball at the "Y," Michi decided to become a volunteer. Soon after he started volunteering, he was immediately hooked on helping other people. He liked the friendly environment, because it satisfied his hunger to help his community.

Michi has accomplished a lot as a volunteer. During the summers, he has been a camp counselor. He enjoys hanging out with kids, playing games, and going on campouts. He even learned how to dance, because some of the kids in the day camp taught him. Michi feels that you can learn many things from younger people.

Michi also was the president of the Teen Leadership Club. This group talked about leadership roles and set up fundraisers. One fundraiser was called a duathalon. A duathalon is a race where the YMCA members run, ride a bike, and then run again. One year, Michi even helped paint the YMCA building.

Besides his volunteer work, Michi got involved in performing arts during high school. When Michi first moved to Washington, he didn't know many people, so he decided to join the class with the most kids in it—the choir. From there he got into the School Show Choir. His choir group traveled all over the area to sing. Some of Michi's other interests include playing the piano and guitar. As you can see, Michi is a very talented person. Michi now attends Evergreen State College, where he studies performing arts such as dancing, acting, and singing. He also does social work and counseling.

A love of music runs in Michi's family. Hiro Imamura and Rae Imamura, two of Michi's aunts, are well-known concert pianists. His grandmother also had musical talent—she wrote songs for the church and played the piano. Michi loves his family. Some of his fondest memories are of family gatherings and his trip to Washington, D.C. There, he and his family visited the Holocaust Memorial and some of the national monuments.

Michi plans to visit Japan soon to experience Buddhism in Japan. This trip will take 2 weeks in the middle of the summer. He plans to spend 1 week in temples and 1 week living with a Japanese family. Michi will be able to communicate with the people, because he took 3 years of Japanese in high school. Michi is very interested in his Japanese Buddhist heritage.

Michi deserved his YMCA Volunteer of the Year award, because he has really made a difference in many lives.

### Tyson Matsumoto

In a room in the State Legislature of Rhode Island, a proposal to change the name of a racist holiday is turned down once again. Tyson Matsumoto and his father, Lloyd, are disappointed. "Victory Over Japan Day" is celebrated on August 14 in Rhode Island. It commemorates the surrender of Japan to the United States to end World War II. Rhode Island is the only state in our coun-

*Tyson Matsumoto*

try that celebrates this holiday. Tyson and other people in the community are not trying to get rid of the holiday, they just want to change the name so that it won't offend any culture or people. For example, he says, a name like "Peace and Remembrance Day" wouldn't single out the Japanese.

Tyson doesn't like seeing what happens on this holiday. Some Asian Americans become victims of racial slurs or worse. Tyson told us about an incident when two women, a Japanese American and a Chinese American, were assaulted as they walked down the street. Sometimes stores owned by any Asians—Korean, Chinese, or Japanese—are vandalized, and their owners are harassed. Tyson feels these things might not happen if the holiday were given a different name.

Tyson's father got him involved in changing the name of the Rhode Island holiday. Tyson himself wrote letters to the *New*

*York Times*, the *Providence Journal*, and the *Barrington Times*. The only paper that actually printed the letter was the *Barrington Times*. Tyson and his father went with others to the State Legislature and presented their idea. But the vote was 12–0 to keep the name of the holiday the same.

The fact that Tyson lives in an area with few Japanese Americans makes it hard for other people to understand his culture and heritage. He lives in Barrington, Rhode Island, and he's 17 years old. Tyson is a freshman at Williams College. He's from a family of four that includes his mother, Terri, his father, Lloyd, and his sister, Carolyn. He wants to visit Japan one day to learn more about his Japanese heritage.

As a child, Tyson dreamed of being a doctor, and that's what he still wants to be. He is volunteering at a local hospital this summer. He wants to attend medical school, so doing well in school has always been one of his priorities. He's received special medals, honors, and awards. He even got one from the President of the United States! Tyson also enjoys playing the violin and being a member of a record-breaking relay team on his high school track team. He hopes to continue these activities in college.

Meanwhile, Tyson's group has tried for many years to bring a change to the name, "Victory Over Japan Day," and every year it is opposed. Tyson says that changing the name of the holiday will probably be put on hold until new lawmakers are voted into office. By then, the community might be more informed about the issue, too.

Tyson's hope for the future is that there

won't be so much racism in our country. In his letter to the *Barrington Times* editor, he wrote: "The most effective method to realize the goal of 'one people' is through education. . . Indeed, learning about the value of cultural diversity would enable people to recognize the similarities that they share with others and to see the differences that make them unique."

### Eri Nakagami

Eri Nakagami is someone who stands up against racism.

Eri was born in Mexico City, Mexico. Her mother, Masako, her father, Tadayuki, and her brother, Ken, were happy to have a new baby. When Eri went to kindergarten in Mexico City, not many Japanese people lived there at the time. She told us that the other kids used to tease the Japanese children by singing songs about them. She handled the teasing by ignoring it and usually they would stop. Her family lived in Mexico for 8 years before moving to Japan. Two years after that, they moved to the United States.

When Eri was a little girl, she wanted to be a doctor. She was born with a heart defect and had open heart surgery. The doctors helped her a lot, so she wanted to save other people's lives in return. She remembers the big party that her family threw for her when she felt better.

In tenth grade, one of Eri's teachers started making remarks about Asians. One thing she remembers her teacher saying is, "Your people are buying out our country." He said some things about how

*Eri Nakagami*

her eyes were slanted and the kind of rice she liked to eat.

At first, Eri tried to ignore the teacher's remarks, but he didn't stop. When she told her parents, they told her to talk to the teacher. Eri decided to do that, and she asked the only other Asian girl in the class to go with her. Unfortunately, the girl came from a strict family, and her father told her to ignore the problem completely.

Finally, Eri went to talk to the teacher by herself. After doing this, nothing changed. The teacher kept saying the same mean remarks. Eri called her seventh grade English teacher, who is also her hero. This teacher told her to stand up for what she believes in and to fight for the rights that she deserves. So Eri went to talk to the principal of her high school. Still, nothing happened.

After waiting for some kind of change in the teacher, Eri took matters into her own hands. She wrote a letter to her school newspaper. Soon, other newspa-

pers got interested. She decided to file a lawsuit against the teacher. Eri was only 16 years old, and she didn't feel she could handle the lawsuit all by herself. It was never settled in court, but the teacher was suspended by the school district.

Since that time, Eri has become more involved with the Japanese American community. She is now a member of two organizations, the Asian Pacific American Network and the National Coalition for Redress and Reparations. She noticed that she was always the youngest person in the group. She tried to get her friends from school to come with her to the meetings, but others did not want to go. Eri is worried about the future of organizations like

these. She believes that if there are no young people getting involved in their cultures, then they will forget their heritage as time goes on.

Eri's goal for the future is to continue to be a part of the Japanese American community. She would also like to go to Ethiopia or another Third World country in the future and help the people there. She would give shots or help in any other way she could. Eri said that if she were unable to go to a different country, she would send money or supplies to the people. For now, she'd like to become a social worker concentrating on working with victims of domestic violence. She would also like to be a mentor for troubled kids.

We asked Eri if she had any advice for kids. She said that we should make education a vital part in our lives, to try to live life to the fullest, and to explore everything—because there is nothing we can't do. Eri told us she was excited about our writing this book and learning more about our heritage. She said she felt a weight come off her shoulders because of our book. She hopes a lot of kids will be inspired to make positive changes.

## Norman Yen

Looking at Norman Yen, you would never guess how many people he has helped. Little does anyone know, this Taiwanese and Japanese American has made a difference in the lives of many people in America's work force. A community activist, Norman lives in California and Providence, Rhode Island, where he stands up for the rights of people who aren't being treated right or who are paid unfairly at their jobs.

Norman grew up in a Latino neighborhood in Los Angeles, California. He was laughed at and teased because he was Asian American, not Latino, like all the other neighborhood kids. Sometimes he would get into fights with those kids, but he always tried to remember that they weren't evil.

Norman was like any other kid growing up. He played baseball, watched television, went to school, and did his homework. School was important to Norman, and he tried hard to get good grades. He grew up celebrating the same holidays as most Americans. He also celebrated some of the Japanese holidays and traditions, such as the anniversaries of relatives' deaths. Norman likes to eat Japanese food, especially the kind served during the Japanese New Year.

Norman's parents taught him many important values. "They have helped me become who I am today," he said. "They have been very supportive." They told him again and again to remember the difference between right and wrong.

Norman met some community activists when he was young. His mother would often take him to her meetings. Her group had worked to expose the government's placement of Japanese Americans in relocation camps during World War II. This is how Norman got interested in working to help others.

When he was young, Norman wanted to be a fireman—or Spiderman. Later, he wanted to be a marine biologist like Jacques Cousteau. Today, Norman wants to enter the medical field to help others, or to become a full-time labor organizer. He is

*Norman Yen (far right) sits with his mother, sister, and grandmother.*

studying to pursue those career interests at Brown University in Providence.

Norman helps with the United Farm Workers organization. Once he was chosen to be in charge of organizing the whole East Coast section of this activist group. This was a great honor for Norman and a great responsibility, too. During this project, he helped the farmers of America get more pay and better treatment. Norman raised money, gave press conferences, and walked the picket lines. Now he is using his summer vacation from college to fight for the rights of hotel workers in California.

Sometimes Norman's job as an activist is very risky for him. He has received strange phone calls from people who disagree with something he has stood for. We're sure that all the people who have worked with Norman Yen would agree that he is a young hero who has made a real difference.

Some of Norman's goals for the future include possibly becoming a doctor or expanding his work as an activist. Who knows? He may even consider writing a book on his work as an activist. Either way, Norman says that he would like to stay in a field where he could continue helping other people. We think helping others makes the right kind of difference!

# STORIES, POETRY, AND LANGUAGE

*Many times we learn a lesson that will last,*
*From things that happened in the past.*
*You can learn a lot from what we have told,*
*Stories, language, haiku, as precious as gold.*

This chapter teaches you all kinds of things about cool stories and interesting books to read. It might also teach you some new words in Japanese or inspire you to write haiku poetry. Read on and learn more about Japanese American stories, poetry, and language.

## FOLK TALES

Cranes, kites, dragons, magic talking animals, and princesses—you can find all this in *mukashi banashi* (moo-kah-shee bah-nah-shee), or Japanese folk tales. Japanese tales are important because they teach valuable lessons. Some of these lessons include being respectful, kind, or helpful and always doing your best.

Children learn Japanese tales in many different ways. They learn them from books, from songs, or at school. During World War II, Japanese American parents and grandparents in the internment camps told the tales aloud to children. Through the generations, as the tales were told and retold, people changed them. So there might be more than 100 ways to tell just one story.

We have found that there are some common features in most Japanese tales. Very

*Young authors and teachers enjoying stories*

old people are often the good characters in the story, because older people are most highly respected in Japanese culture. Not every tale has a happy ending, which is different from many American and European fairy tales. But the two folk tales we have included have happy endings. They are about animals, jokes, and ordinary people and places.

There are more than 15,000 Japanese folk tales and legends, which is more than any country in the Western part of the world has collected. Many of them have been told by more than one author. Sometimes one folk tale is retold by several authors in different books. In our book, we only have room to retell three folk tales. If you like these, you can always go to the library and find more. Here are three tales we read. We hope you like them as much as we did.

## Momotaro, the Peach Boy

*This folk tale is known by most Japanese American kids. They hear it from their grandparents or parents. Some read it in books of folk tales. Others may learn it from the song "Momotaro." This is a popular folk tale in Japan, too. We learned it by reading the book* Momotaro, The Peach Boy, *retold and illustrated by Linda Shute (New York: Lathrop, Lee, and Shepard Books, 1986).*

Once upon a time in old Japan, there lived an old couple who prayed for a child to take care of them in their old age. One day, the old woman was washing clothes in the river, when she saw a gigantic peach float-

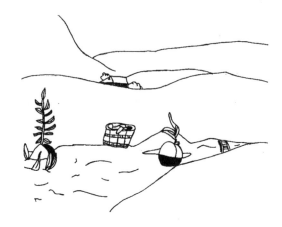

ing in the river. She reached out and lifted the peach into her laundry basket to take home for dinner.

"Boy, am I ever hungry," her husband announced when he came home from cutting wood. He wanted to cut the peach the instant his wife showed it to him. All of a sudden, a voice came from the peach, saying, "Don't cut! Don't cut!"

"Gracious!" said the old woman.

The peach split open and a baby boy popped out. The old man and woman said, "You were brought from heaven to answer our prayers. We will call you Momotaro, which means 'peach boy.'"

The parents gave him love and care. With every meal he got stronger and bigger. When Momotaro was full-grown, he decided to go to the island of the oni, who were vicious and greedy creatures that stole from others. His parents sadly gave him their blessings.

The next day, he set off on his journey with his sword, a banner with his peach emblem on it, an iron war fan, and three

the wall and unlocked the gate. Momotaro sneaked up on the oni. He yelled, "We are here to get the stolen goods back for our village people."

"You must be kidding. We are not afraid of you," yelled the vicious oni king.

The battle against the oni began. The dog bit at their ankles, the monkey pulled their ears, the pheasant pecked at their eyes and heads, and Momotaro used his sword to fight the oni. The oni were so confused that they thought they were fighting a large army. The oni king surrendered and gave back the stolen treasures.

Momotaro and his friends brought the treasures back to the villagers. At Momotaro's home, they had the best kibi dango in all of Japan, and they all lived happily ever after.

## Three Strong Women

*We learned this tale from reading the book* Three Strong Women: A Tall Tale from Japan, *by Claus Stamm, illustrated by Jean and Mou-sien Tseng (New York: Viking Penguin, 1990).*

There once was a wrestler named Forever Mountain who thought he was very strong. On his way to the emperor's wrestling match, he saw a girl named Marume carrying a bucket of water on her head. He wanted to make her laugh and drop the bucket, so he could fill it up for her and show off his strength. When Forever Mountain tickled Marume, she trapped his hand underneath her arm. Forever Mountain was sure he could get away, but he was stuck.

*kibi dango*, which are rice dumplings. He sat down to eat one of his kibi dango, when a skinny dog came along and said, "I am starving!"

Momotaro felt sorry for the dog and said, "I can do without one kibi dango." So he gave one to the hungry dog.

The grateful dog decided to help Momotaro fight his battle with the oni. Soon they saw a monkey and a pheasant. Momotaro gave them his last two kibi dango. The kibi dango made them stronger, and they too decided to join Momotaro.

The four friends went over the mountain and reached the ocean. They got onto a boat and headed toward the island of the oni. When they got there, Momotaro told the pheasant to fly above the wall and spy on the oni. The monkey climbed over

"You're hurting my hand. Please let go!" he begged.

Marume said, "I'll let you go if you come to my house. My grandmother, my mom, and I will help you get stronger for the wrestling match. Our amazing strength will surprise you."

Forever Mountain followed Marume to her home. There, he trained by doing the work of many men, carrying heavy loads such as cows, gigantic buckets of water, and large bundles of wood. He wrestled with the grandmother each night. Finally, after 3 months of training, he could hold the old woman down for 30 seconds! He had grown very fond of the family, and asked Marume to marry him when he returned from the wrestling match.

At the competition, Forever Mountain beat the first man just by stamping on his foot. Everyone was scared. No one would go against him, so he won the prize money. The emperor made him promise not to wrestle anymore, because he was so much stronger than the rest. Forever Mountain returned and became a farmer and married Marume. They all lived happily ever after.

## How the Withered Trees Blossomed

*We learned this story from a book made the way books in Japan are made. It opens on the left, rather than on the right like books do in our country. Each page of this book includes an illustration and the story in both English and Japanese Hiragana characters. Japanese writing starts on the right and goes left, instead of left to right, like ours, and it is written from the top to the bottom of the page. This book was written by Miyoko Matsutani and illustrated by Yasuo Segawa (Philadelphia: Lippincott, 1969).*

A long time ago, there was a kind old couple living in the country. One day, the old man went fishing and put his fishing basket in the river. His mean neighbor saw the kind old man and put his own fishing basket upstream, so that he would catch all the fish before they swam into the kind old man's basket.

The next day, the mean neighbor went to see if he had caught any fish, but all he had in his basket was a thick old root. He said in an angry voice, "All I caught was a crummy root!" The mean neighbor then went to the kind old man's basket and

saw that he had a basketful of fish. He stole the fish and put his old root into the old man's basket.

When the old man went to check his basket and saw the old root, he said, "At least I caught something. I can use this root for firewood." He took the root home to split and dry it. But when he split the root, a cute little white puppy jumped out of it! The old couple named the puppy Shiro, which means "white."

They fed Shiro and loved him, and he grew bigger and bigger. One day, Shiro really surprised the old couple when he started talking. He said, "Put a saddle and straw bag on me and bring a spade, then hop onto my back."

The old man said, "Oh no, I can't do that! I'm too heavy for you and I will break your back!"

But Shiro answered, "No, you won't. Just do what I say." So the old man did.

Shiro took the old man up into the mountains and told him to dig in a special spot. The old man did exactly as the dog told him to do.

While the old man was digging, his spade hit precious gems and gold that were buried there. He put them in the straw bags and took them home to show his wife. They emptied the bags into big piles of gold and jewels and joyfully played with them. The mean neighbor heard the "clink, clink, clink" of the gold and ran over to see where the kind man had found the treasure.

After the kind man told him how he got the gold, the mean neighbor asked to borrow Shiro. The mean man and his wife beat Shiro and forced him to show them where to dig. When the old man started digging, all he found were snakes, worms, and dirt. "You made us feel ridiculous!" yelled the mean old man. He beat Shiro with the spade and killed him.

The mean couple buried Shiro in the mountains and planted a willow tree in the spot. They went back to the kind old couple's house and told them what had happened. The kind old couple sobbed and missed Shiro very much.

The next day, the kind old man went up into the mountains to visit the spot where the dog was buried and saw that the willow tree had grown. The old man cut off a branch to take home to remember Shiro.

At home, he carved a bowl out of the wood. When the old couple ground rice in the bowl, the rice turned into gold. The mean old woman came over to see what all the racket was about. After they told her what had happened, she borrowed the bowl. When she took the bowl home and ground her rice in it, all she got was yucky, stinky dirt. She was so mad that she burned the bowl and returned the ashes to the kind neighbors. The neighbors were very sad, because the bowl was a treasure to them to remember Shiro.

The kind old man decided to spread the ashes on the crab apple trees in his yard, and the trees magically bloomed with beautiful pink blossoms. His yard was gorgeous!

A prince rode by and saw the beautiful yard. "I will reward you for making the withered trees blossom," he said. "Those crab apple trees are so pretty!"

Then the mean neighbor grabbed the ashes from the old man and said, "I am the man who can make the trees more beautiful." But when he threw the ashes, they went right into the prince's eyes. The prince got so mad that he told his guards to beat the mean neighbor. The mean neighbor had to run for his life and leave his home.

The kind old couple bought some new white puppies to remind them of Shiro, and they all lived happily ever after.

## BOOKS

Books are lots of fun because they teach us many things we didn't know and help us to enjoy the world in a new way. We read many books of stories written by Japanese American authors. In this section, we tell some of our very favorite stories in our own words.

### Baseball Saved Us

*This is the story of how a Japanese American boy's love for baseball helped him* *survive the time he spent in an internment camp. (See the history chapter for more information on internment camps.) This book was written by Ken Mochizuki and illustrated by Dom Lee (New York: Lee and Low, 1993).*

In the camps, it was hot and dusty in the summer, and cold and windy in the winter. The guards had guns and watched the people all the time. People in the camps became sad, bored, and angry.

One boy's father decided to make a baseball field to help people forget about their sadness and anger. The grownups and the kids all helped pull up the sagebrush to clear the field near the barracks where they lived. The guard in the tower watched them work every day.

Soon the field was ready, and the baseball games began, with grownups and kids playing together. All summer, the Japanese Americans played baseball, which became a big event in the camp. The whole time, the guard continued to watch. The boy whose father decided to make the baseball field was not a very good player, and everyone always made fun of him. But he never gave up.

During the last game of the season, his team was in the championships, and they were losing by one point. The boy came up to bat. He heard the other team hollering, "Easy out!" As the other team teased him, the boy looked up and saw the sun glinting off the guard's sunglasses. The boy was so sick of being watched by guards all the time that he got angry and really whacked the ball with all his might. His home run won the game, and everyone cheered for him! Even the guard in the tower smiled and gave him a thumbs-up sign.

You may think this is a happy ending to the story, but remember that the Japanese Americans were still held in the camp. Finally, the Japanese Americans were allowed to go, and the boy returned to his old school. It was bad before he went to camp, but now it was even worse. Children called him mean names like "Jap."

Later in the year, the boy joined a baseball team at his school. The kids at school thought he was an "easy out," too. One day at a game, the crowd was shouting, "The Jap's no good!" As the boy stepped up to bat, he looked over at the pitcher and saw the sun glint off his glasses and remembered the guard in the tower. The boy got really angry again and swung the bat with all his might. He hit the ball and watched it sail over the fence once again.

### Crow Boy

*This story is about a boy who was made fun of because he did things differently. Some people didn't want to read this book, because it has a picture of a person on the front that isn't drawn very well. This book taught us an important lesson—the one teachers always tell us: "Never judge a*

*book by its cover." We decided to give the book a try. We really liked reading it and hope you do, too. If you judge a book by its cover, you might miss out on something wonderful inside. This book is by Taro Yashima (New York: Viking Press, 1983).*

Once there was a little boy in Japan called Chibi, which means "little boy." Chibi was not well liked at his school. He was always left alone to eat and to play, and he stood at the end of every line. Chibi didn't try to make any friends, and he pretended not to listen to his teachers. He picked up gross bugs that no one else would even look at, and everyone thought he was strange. His classmates and the grownups called him stupid and slow-poke. Chibi learned how to cross his eyes, so that he wouldn't have to see the mean and ugly faces other kids made at him.

Finally, Chibi got a nice sixth grade teacher, Mr. Isobe, who really liked him a lot. Mr. Isobe took the class on many field trips. Chibi knew a lot about the flowers in the garden, and he knew where wild grapes and potatoes grew. This made Mr. Isobe very happy. Mr. Isobe even talked with Chibi when nobody was around.

One day, Chibi's school had a talent show. When Chibi stood on the stage, everyone said, "Why is Chibi up there? He is too stupid to do anything."

Mr. Isobe told the audience that Chibi would make the voices of crows. First, Chibi made the voice of a newly hatched crow. Next, he made the voices of mother and father crows. Finally, he made the

sound of the crows that lived near his home. The sounds he made were so lonely that they made everyone sad. When Chibi was done, the audience clapped and had tears in their eyes, because they remembered how badly they had treated Chibi. Mr. Isobe told everyone how far Chibi had to walk to school every day, and that while he walked, Chibi listened to the crow calls.

After that, everyone felt differently about Chibi. They understood him better. On graduation day, Chibi was the only student with perfect attendance for all 6 years. From that day on, no one called him Chibi, they called him Crow Boy. He really liked his new name, and whenever he walked, he would make the voice of a happy crow.

## OTHER GOOD BOOKS

Here are a few suggestions for more Japanese and Japanese American stories and folk tales we liked. Read them and you might like them, too!

• *A to Zen*, by Ruth Wells, illustrated by Yoshi (Saxonville: Picture Book Studio, 1992). Using the letters of the English alphabet, *A to Zen* describes 26 Japanese words. This book opens on the left, like a traditional Japanese book, opposite to the way Western books are opened.

• *The Badger and the Magic Fan*, by Tony Johnston, illustrated by Tomie dePaola (New York: Putnam, 1990). This book is

about a mean badger who tricks the *tengu* (tehn-goo), or goblin children, into giving him a magic fan. By the end of the book, the badger ends up wishing he had never played the trick.

• *Faithful Elephants*, by Yukio Tsuchiya, illustrated by Ted Lewin (Boston: Houghton Mifflin, 1988). This is a true story of three elephants in the Tokyo zoo that were killed because the zookeepers were afraid all the dangerous animals would run wild through the city during the war.

• *Mouse's Marriage*, written and illustrated by Junko Morimoto (New York: Viking Penguin, 1986). A mouse is looking for a husband who is the mightiest in the world. Her search is long and tiring, but she finally finds the best husband.

• *A Pair of Red Clogs*, written by Masako Matsuno, illustrated by Kazue Mizumura (New York: World Publishing Co., 1960). A girl gets a brand new pair of red clogs. When one clog gets cracked while she plays a game, she tries to trick her mother into getting her a new pair.

• *The Paper Crane*, by Molly Bang (New York: Greenwillow Books, 1985). A poor restaurant owner gets a magic paper crane that comes to life and dances for his customers.

• *The Rooster Who Understood Japanese*, by Yoshiko Uchida, illustrated by Charles Robinson (New York: Charles Scribner's Sons, 1976). This is a story of an old woman who has many pets, including a rooster named Mr. Lincoln who understands Japanese.

• *Sachiko Means Happiness*, by Kimiko Sakai, illustrated by Tomie Arai (San Francisco: Children's Book Press, 1990). This story is about a girl named Sachiko, which means "happiness." Her grandmother has Alzheimer's disease and thinks she is a little girl again.

• *Sadako and the Thousand Paper Cranes*, written by Eleanor Coerr, paintings by Ronald Himler (New York: Dell Publishing, 1977). There are many books about the atom bomb that was dropped on Hiroshima, Japan, during World War II. This book is probably the best-known of them. It is the true story of a girl who was affected by the bomb.

• *The Stonecutter*, written and illustrated by Gerald McDermott (New York: Penguin, 1978). Tasaku wishes to become many things, but he discovers his own foolishness.

• *Tree of Cranes*, written and illustrated by Allen Say (Boston: Houghton Mifflin, 1991). A young boy in Japan learns the story of an important American holiday. The book also has very beautiful illustrations.

More books are coming out all the time, so ask your librarians for good books about Japanese American heritage. Remember to tell them about this book written by kids, too!

## HAIKU

*Haiku* (hy-koo) is a form of poetry that is nearly 300 years old. Each haiku has 17 syllables. The first and third lines of a haiku have five syllables, and the second line has seven.

Haiku poets write about seasons and nature, but you can write about anything you like. Whatever you choose to write about, your haiku should make readers see what you're writing about in a new and different way. Remember, haikus don't have to rhyme.

Here is an easy way to get started on your haiku:

1. Pick a topic to write about.
2. Write as many five and seven syllable lines about your topic as you can think of.

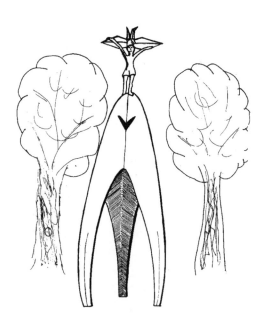

3. Choose your favorite five-syllable line for the first line of your haiku.
4. Choose your favorite seven-syllable line for the second line.
5. Choose another five-syllable line for the third line.

You have just written your own haiku! Here are some we wrote:

*Big, bright, full colors*
*soaring up into the wind,*
*kites fly high and proud.*

♦ ♦ ♦

*Festive, happy, hot,*
*dancing, eating together*
*on a July night.*

♦ ♦ ♦

*The wind is screaming.*
*It makes the trees blow crazy,*
*makes them fall apart.*

♦ ♦ ♦

*Elegant seagull*
*flies through the air gracefully*
*far above the clouds.*

♦ ♦ ♦

*Water is dripping,*
*a puddle of water on*
*the pretty flowers.*

## LANGUAGE

We learned a lot about the Japanese language, especially about the different ways of writing Japanese. We'll teach you some words and expressions in Japanese—even the Japanese names and sounds of certain animals!

### Japanese Language School

When they were kids, many Nisei, Sansei, and Yonsei went to *Nihongakko* (nee-hohn-gah-koh), Japanese language school. Some went on Saturdays, some on Sundays, and some even went after their regular school during the week. The classes were held at Buddhist temples, community centers, and Japanese American churches.

At Nihongakko, children learned Japanese words, origami, songs, folk tales, and how to write Japanese characters. Some Nihongakko even had recitals, so the children could show their parents what they had learned.

Parents had their children attend Nihongakko, because they wanted them to learn about their Japanese heritage. Some of the children didn't like it, but they did like meeting new friends. Today, many Sansei and Yonsei parents still send their children to Nihongakko.

## Writing Japanese

Did you know that there are three ways to write in Japanese? They are *kanji* (kan-gee), *hiragana* (hee-rah-gah-nah), and *katakana* (kah-tah-kah-nah).

Kanji is used for formal writing and signs. Kanji characters were adapted from Chinese characters. It is the most difficult kind of writing to learn in Japan, because each kanji character is a stick-figure picture of what it represents. A kanji character sometimes stands for a whole word. Only about 2,000 kanji are used regularly, but there are more than 45,000 in a complete dictionary. Here are examples of some kanji characters:

This is *ki* (kee), the word for "tree." Can you see the roots of the tree in this word?

When you put lots of trees together, you get the word *mori* (moh-ree), which means "forest." Can you see all the trees in the forest?

This is *hito* (hee-toh), the Kanji word for "person." Can you see the body and legs of a walking person?

The second style of writing is hiragana. It is used more in everyday life and is easier to write than kanji. Hiragana is like an alphabet because, to create a word from it, you need more than one character.

The last form is katakana. This is used for the words that were not originally used by the Japanese. Such words could be foreign words brought to Japan, such as "hamburger," or someone's name in English, French, or another language.

It is not very hard to pronounce Japanese words. The five vowels are always pronounced the same way, like this:

a = "ah" as in "father"
e = "eh" as in "get"
i = "ee" as in "machine"
o = "oh" as in "hope"
u = "oo" as in "flu"

## Counting In Japanese

We all know how to count from one to ten, but do you know how to count in Japanese? There are several ways. Here's one:

one = *ichi* (ee-chee)
two = *ni* (nee)
three = *san* (sahn)
four = *shi* (shee)
five = *go* (goh)
six = *roku* (ro-koo)
seven = *shichi* (shee-chee)
eight = *hachi* (hah-chee)
nine = *ku* (koo)
ten = *ju* (joo)

## Animals and Their Sounds

Have you ever wondered what animals are called in Japanese? Did you know that in Japanese dogs don't say "bow-wow," they say "wan-wan"? We thought you might be interested to learn the names and sounds of animals in Japanese. See the box below.

| ENGLISH | | JAPANESE | |
|---|---|---|---|
| **Animal** | **Sound** | **Animal** | **Sound** |
| dog | bow-wow | *inu* (ee-noo) | *wan-wan* (wahn-wahn) |
| cat | meow | *neko* (neh-koh) | *nya* (nyah) |
| frog | ribbet | *kaeru* (kah-eh-roo) | *kero-kero* (keh-roh keh-roh) |
| cow | moo | *ushi* (oo-shee) | *mo* (moh) |
| pig | oink | *buta* (boo-tah) | *bu* (boo) |
| sheep | baa | *hitsuji* (hee-tsoo-jee) | *me* (meh) |
| rooster | cock-a-doodle-doo | *ondori* (ohn-doh-ree) | *koke kokko* (koh-keh kohk-koh) |
| bird | cheep cheep | *tori* (toh-ree) | *chi chi* (chee-chee) |
| mouse | squeak | *nezumi* (neh-zoo-mee) | *chu chu* (choo-choo) |
| duck | quack | *ahiru* (ah-hee-roo) | *kuwa kuwa* (koo-wah, koo-wah) |

## Expressions and Salutations

These are words you will want to know if you wish to speak Japanese. In fact, many Japanese Americans use these expressions and greetings here in America.

good day—*konnichi wa* (kohn-nee-chee wah)

good evening—*konban wa* (kohn-bahn wah)

good morning—*ohayo gozaimasu* (oh-hah-yo goh-zah-ee-mah-su)

good night—*oyasumi nasai* (o-yah-soo-mee nah-sigh)

good-bye—*sayonara* (sah-yoh-nah-rah)

thank you—*domo arigato gozaimasu* (doh-moh ah-ree-gah-toh goh-zah-ee-mah-su)

you're welcome—*do itashimashite* (doh ee-tah-shee-mahsh-teh)

I'm sorry—*gomen nasai* (goh-mehn nah-sigh)

how are you?—*genki desu ka* (gehn-kee dehs-ka)

I'm fine—*genki des* (gehn-kee dehs)

I'm happy—*ureshi* (oo-reh-shee)

I'm sad—*kanashi* (kah-nah-shee)

let's go—*ikimasho* (ee-kee-mah-shoh)

tough it out—*gaman* (gah-mahn)

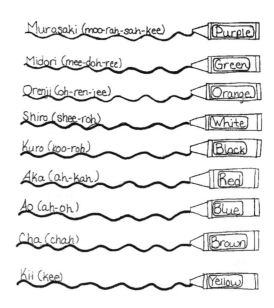

Murasaki (moo-rah-sah-kee) — Purple

Midori (mee-doh-ree) — Green

Orenji (oh-ren-jee) — Orange

Shiro (shee-roh) — White

Kuro (koo-roh) — Black

Aka (ah-kah) — Red

Ao (ah-oh) — Blue

Cha (chah) — Brown

Kii (kee) — Yellow

The next time you hear or see these words, you will know they come from the Japanese language.

## Borrowed Words

Some English words have made it into the Japanese language, just as some Japanese words have entered into English. Here are a few examples:

baseball—*beisuboru*
Batman—*Battoman*
boss—*bosu*
Coca-Cola—*Koka Koura*
coffee—*kohi*
hamburger—*hanbaga*
hot dog—*hotto doggu*

The young authors interviewing the storyteller

## Common Japanese Words

Did you know that Americans use Japanese words in TV commercials, restaurants, stores, and in some of the phrases we use? Here are a few examples:

- We've seen different *dojos,* or martial arts schools, around the city that teach *karate, judo,* and *kendo.*
- Some stores sell *zoris,* or thongs, every summer. Some stores also sell beautiful *kimonos,* or long robes.
- We've heard people say *"Sayonara"* to each other to say good-bye.
- Many bedding and furniture stores here sell *futon* beds.
- *Sushi*, *tempura*, and *teriyaki* are the names of some of the foods served in Japanese (and American) restaurants.
- Nowadays, *karaoke* singing is popular in nightclubs, restaurants, and at parties. Karaoke singers get up on stage and sing along to a taped song.

Chris Tucker

McDonalds—*Makudonarudo*
orange—*orenji*
Pepsi—*Pepushi*
pizza—*piza*
rocket—*roketto*
salad—*sarada*
spaghetti—*supaggeti*
Walkman—*Wokuman*

We hope you have enjoyed learning about Japanese stories, poetry, and language. Remember, there are many more books at the library for you to read on these subjects.

# HANDS-ON FUN

*You can cook, play games, and make crafts, too,*
*And do things that are fun for you.*
*You can learn to do things the Japanese way,*
*And brighten any gloomy day.*

In this chapter, you'll learn how to make some crafts, play new games, make gifts for your friends, and cook a few favorite Japanese American recipes. We enjoyed doing these things in our workshop, because they have been done by children and adults for hundreds of years. We learned that we have a lot in common with kids from long ago, no matter what our backgrounds are.

## CRAFTS

### Origami

Origami (oh-ree-gah-mee) is the art of paper folding. It started in Japan more than 600 years ago, and many Americans enjoy this hobby today. All you do is follow directions to fold paper many times in different shapes, until it turns into what you are trying to make. You learn to concentrate, read, and follow directions—and be patient.

When you do origami, you are also learning geometry because you are making shapes while you are folding paper. Origami paper always starts out as a square, and it comes in different colors. One side of the

*Learning the art of origami*

Chris Tucker

Chris Tucker

*Having fun with origami hats*

paper is usually white and the other side is either a solid color or a colored design.

Many people like to make cranes out of origami paper, because the crane is a special symbol for many things. It is a symbol of peace and long life. It's also a sign of good health. Some people believe cranes will make miracles happen and make your dreams come true.

Japanese Americans sometimes give their daughters or sons 1,000 origami cranes in red, gold, or silver to wish them good luck when they get married. The most popular color for wedding cranes is gold. Some families also make 1,000 gold cranes for a 50th wedding anniversary.

When doing origami, you get to enjoy the beauty of what you make. It also feels good to finish something and be able to follow directions. Practicing origami can help make the muscles in your fingers stronger and teach you to move them gracefully. We give origami two thumbs up!

There are many books on origami that tell you how to make a crane. After you learn

to do this, try making 1,000 cranes with your friends or family. This would be a good project for a rainy day. Then give them to someone on an important occasion.

## Darumas

The *daruma* (dah-roo-mah) is a popular Japanese figure, sort of like a little doll. It stands for inner strength, determination, and perseverance. It was named after Bodhidharma, a Zen priest. He sat and meditated for a long, long time. After doing this, he lost the use of his arms and legs. Many legends say that he then rolled himself through China to teach.

The daruma is a little egg-shaped figure with a weight in the bottom so it will pop back up like a punching bag. You might think the daruma's face looks angry, but it's not. It's a look of determination.

Many think the daruma is a good-luck charm against illness and bad fortune. Some people think of a goal they want to

achieve. Then they draw the outline of eyes on the daruma but fill in only one eye. When their goal or wish comes true, they fill in the other eye. But for the wish to come true, they have to work hard.

We're glad this idea came from Japan to America. Some of us are painting one eye, and our goal is to make good grades. We will keep working, even though it is hard. Just like the daruma, no matter which way you push us, we will pop back up.

When you make something, always keep in mind what it will look like in the end. A daruma has the shape of an egg with a flat bottom. Look at the picture and think about what you want yours to look like. To make a daruma, you will need a plastic sandwich bag, strips of paper, liquid starch, plaster of paris, and colored paints.

1. To begin, stuff a plastic sandwich bag with strips of crumpled paper until it is very full.

2. Fold the top of the bag over and tape it shut. This is also the time to tape the corners of the bag and try to form an egg shape with a flat bottom.

3. Draw a 1-inch circle on the top of the bag. We will cut out this circle later and use the hole to remove the paper.

4. Take a strip of newspaper 1 inch wide and 6 inches long, and dip it in liquid starch. Wrap it around the plastic bag, but don't cover the hole. Do this again and again, until the whole bag is covered with four or five layers of papier-mâché.

5. As you put on the layers, remember to

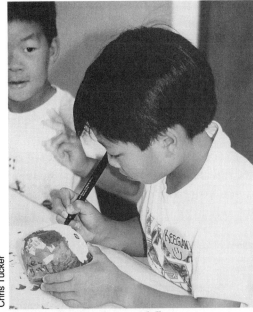

*Painting faces on daruma dolls*

work on the shape. Look at the picture to see what shape the daruma has. Make sure it's flat on the bottom, so it will stand up.

6. After it has dried overnight, cut out the circle on top and pull out the paper from inside the plastic bag.

*A collection of daruma dolls*

7. When all the newspaper is out, pour about a half-inch of plaster of paris in the bottom to make it heavy. Cover the top with more papier mâché, and then let it dry until it is hard.

8. When it is dry, paint the face white and the body red. After that has dried, decorate the face with black and gold.

9. Color in one eye and make a wish or set a goal. When your wish comes true or when you have met your goal, color in the other eye.

This project is fun because your daruma makes you try to reach your goal. When both of the eyes are colored in, it helps you remember your success. You might want to make one as a gift for a friend's birthday or graduation.

## Kites

Thousands of years ago, the very first kite was flown in China. From there, the idea soon spread to Japan. The Japanese word for "kite" is *tako* (tah-koh), which also means "octopus." Can you guess why this was chosen for the word "kite"?

People all over the world enjoy flying kites. You can see them on beaches and in parks, open fields, and meadows. Kite flying is a popular sport for all ages, from kids to adults. Today's kites range from the hand-held ones to remote control kites. There are giant kites that weigh more than 1,700 pounds and take 50 people to fly them. Other kites are as small as postage stamps. Some people can even fly five or more kites at the same time. It's fun just

Chris Tucker

*A Japanese kite*

to sit and watch beautiful kites soar gracefully in the sky.

Kites are made out of many different materials, but the one thing they have in common is that they are very colorful. We found an easy way to make a kite that really flies. You will need a white plastic trash bag that you can draw a picture on. You might want to draw a picture of a *samurai* (a Japanese warrior), or you can use fairy-tale characters, animals, or nature scenes to decorate your kite.

Here are the directions for making a kite:

1. Cut out your kite according to the measurements shown in the picture.

2. Tape two 16-inch dowels (thin, round sticks) to the left and right sides of the bag.

3. Make a design or draw a picture with permanent markers so it doesn't rub off. Make your kite colorful.

4. Put several pieces of tape on corners 1 and 2 to make them strong.

5. Poke a hole in these corners with something sharp. Be careful not to hurt yourself.

6. Cut a string twice as wide as your kite.

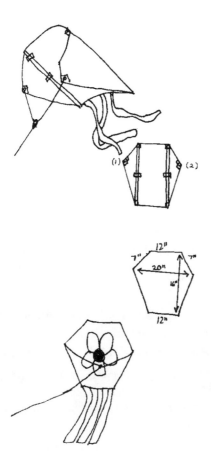

In the middle of the string, tie a small loop. Then put the string through the holes you made at 1 and 2, so that the loop is in the middle of one side of the kite.

7. Tie the ends of this string together on the other side of the kite.

8. Tie the end of a long kite string to the little loop in the middle of the string that goes through the holes at 1 and 2.

9. Tape three rag tails or crepe paper strips to the bottom of the kite. Then wait for a windy day and see how easy it is to fly this kite.

## Carp Wind Socks

Wind socks are cloth tubes, open at both ends, that hang outside and wave in the wind. In America, you can buy wind socks in many different shapes and sizes. In recent years, they have become very popular and can be seen flying from balconies, porches, and patios. Carp wind socks might be seen during a Japanese American festival.

The carp is a fish that is important in Japanese culture. Read the Boys' Day section in the chapter entitled "Culture and the Arts" to learn the legend of a boy named Kintaro and how he fought with a man-eating carp. You'll also find out why families often fly several carp wind socks of different sizes on Boys' Day.

We think wind socks are fun and easy to make. Here's how to make a carp wind sock.

You will need some cloth. Old white sheets or muslin are best. You will also need scissors, thread or fabric glue, markers or felt pens in different colors, a pipe cleaner, wax paper, and string.

1. Cut your cloth in the shape of a carp. See the picture on the next page.

2. Make a 1-inch fold at the flat tip of the carp, insert a pipe cleaner in the fold, and then glue the mouth of the carp with the pipe cleaner still in the fold.

3. Fold your carp in half the long way. Then twist the ends of the pipe cleaner together. Insert wax paper in between the fold so that the paint won't go through

Chris Tucker

*Making a carp wind sock*

onto the other side. Glue or sew the edges of the carp together, leaving the mouth and tail section open so the wind can get inside.

4. Decorate your carp using felt pens or poster paint. You can decorate your wind sock with paint brushes, or use sponges cut

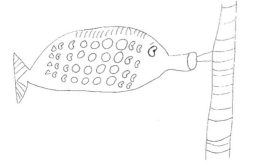

in a kidney shape to sponge-paint the scales. Use any extra material to make fins or streamers on the end.

5. When your design is dry, tie a heavy string to the mouth so your carp can fly.

The best part about making a carp wind sock is decorating it. You can be as creative as you want to be. When each of our kites was displayed, we knew exactly which one was ours.

## GAMES

In this section, you'll find games you play the Japanese American way. We played these games and think you will like them.

### Go

*Go* means "five" in Japanese. In Japan, Go is the most popular indoor game, and it can be very complex. It is played by some Japanese American children. We played Go and enjoyed it.

This is how to play. You use a rectangular checkerboard of 20 inches by 19 inches, set up with 19 lines up and down and 19 lines across. Two people take turns putting tokens on the board at any point where the lines cross, until someone gets five in a row.

The rows can be in any direction. As you play, you try to block the other person from getting five in a row first. Go is like the American game "Connect Four." Like Connect Four, you have to think fast and use different strategies to play Go.

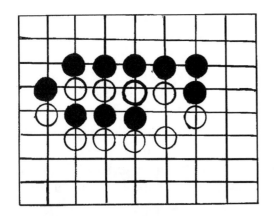

ican game called *Jan Ken Po* that is very similar. Instead of "1, 2, 3", you say "Jan Ken Po," which is a way to decide whose turn is next, sort of like "eenie, meenie, miney, moe." The name of the game comes from the word *ken*, which means "fist." Here's how to play. First, pick out a friend to play with you. Shake your fist three times in the air. The first time you shake your fist, say "Jan." The second time, say "Ken." The

## Bean Go

Bean Go is like Go. You use the same board and the same tokens, but in Bean Go you put your tokens inside the squares and then surround the other person's tokens. While you play, your partner tries to surround your tokens. Once you surround the other person's tokens, you take them. The winner is the person who gets all of the other player's tokens.

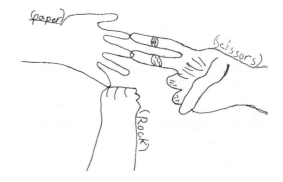

Chris Tucker

*Young authors learning to play Bean Go*

## Jan Ken Po

Have you ever played the game "rock, scissors, paper"? Well, there is a Japanese Amer-

last time, say "Po," and make a fist for rock, open hand for paper, or a V for scissors. Remember—the rock breaks the scissors, the paper covers the rock, and the scissors cut the paper.

## Hashi Kyoso

To play *Hashi Kyoso* (hah-shee kyoh-soh), you will need a cup for each player, a pair of hashi (chopsticks), and something to pick up, like peanuts or marshmallows. You will need two or more people to play. The idea is to have a contest to see who can get all the marshmallows out of the cup first by getting one out at a time using only

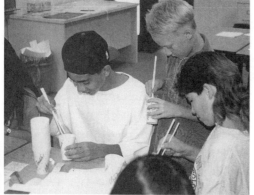

Chris Tucker

*Playing Hashi Kyoso*

the chopsticks. This game will be easier if you learn to use the chopsticks by reading the section in this chapter entitled "How to Use Hashi."

Another good way to play this game is to see who can eat the marshmallows or peanuts faster. Anyone can play this game. The point of this game is to teach you to use chopsticks. It's lots of fun.

## RECIPES

Japanese Americans believe that food should look as good as it tastes. Each serving is put in a separate dish to keep the tastes from mixing. Japanese American cooking usually uses the freshest ingredients and cooks them for only a short time. The recipes also use meat only in small amounts. The Japanese style of cooking is said to be one of the healthiest in the world.

The most common Japanese food is rice. Noodles are also popular. We liked all the different kinds of noodles. *Soba* (soh-bah)

are brown noodles made from buckwheat. *Udon* (oo-dohn), or winter noodles, and *somen* (soh-men), or summer noodles, are made from wheat flour. They may be served hot or cold. They can be eaten as a quick snack, like an apple or a sandwich. Many soybean products are used, too, such as soy sauce, *miso* (mee-soh) (soybean paste), and *tofu* (toh-foo), which is soybean curd. These are important parts of Japanese American cooking.

The recipes included in this section show the importance of the changing seasons. These recipes are easy to prepare and the ingredients can be found easily. The average cooking time for the recipes is about 45 minutes.

Other recipes, such as *teriyaki, sashimi* (raw fish), and *tempura* (vegetables or seafood fried in a special batter), were not included, because they are too hard for kids to make or cost too much money.

Even though cooking the food is fun, eating it is the best part! We would like to teach you how to use *hashi*—chopsticks—

Chris Tucker

*Learning to cook Japanese American recipes*

to eat your food. Some people don't know there is a difference between Japanese and Chinese chopsticks. Japanese hashi are smaller and thinner than Chinese chopsticks. If you want a fun way to practice using hashi, play the game Hashi Kyoso from the games section.

## How to Use Hashi

1. Rest one of the hashi between your middle finger and thumb. Curl your index finger over the top as though you were using a pencil.
2. Pinch the other hashi between your index finger and thumb. Push your index finger down and keep the bottom hashi straight with your thumb. Keep the hashi ends even.
3. Chow down!

## Dashi

*Dashi* (dah-shee) is a soup base for many dishes in Japanese American cooking. Many recipes start with dashi. Dashi is used for all Japanese American noodles. You will find that you'll use this recipe frequently while cooking.

6 cups water
5-6 teaspoons *hon dashi* (concentrated soup base)

Boil water. Add hon dashi. Stir.

## Somen

Somen, also called summer noodles, is very good as a main dish or as a snack. You can eat this with chopsticks or a fork. Somen noodles are good in the summertime, especially when the weather is hot, because they are cold and can cool you off. This recipe is easy. It serves eight people.

### Somen Noodles

2 lbs. somen noodles

Toppings: green onions, *kamaboko* (kah-mah-boh-koh) (pressed fish cake), hard-boiled eggs, *nori* (noh-ree) (dried seaweed), or cucumber.

In a large saucepan, bring water to a boil. Add somen noodles. Cook 3 minutes. Do not overcook. Drain in a colander and run cold water over them. Set aside. You also need somen sauce for this dish.

### Somen Sauce

6 cups dashi
½ cup *mirin* (mee-reen) (Japanese sweet rice wine used for cooking)
½ cups *shoyu* (soy sauce)

In a large saucepan, combine all ingredients. Boil mixture and then refrigerate sauce until you're ready to serve the dish. To serve, put the noodles in small bowls and pour some sauce over them, then add toppings.

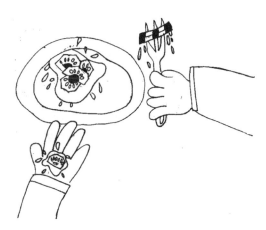

## Sunomono

*Sunomono* (soo-noh-moh-noh) is cucumber salad. This dish has both a sweet and salty taste to it. Many of us liked the mix of sugar and salt together. The sauce is a mixture of soy sauce, rice vinegar, and sugar. This recipe is easy to make and doesn't take too much time. It serves four people.

    2   cucumbers, sliced thin
    ¼   cup sugar
    ¼   cup rice vinegar
    ¼   teaspoon salt
    ¼   teaspoon soy sauce

Cut off ends of the cucumber. Peel the cucumber in alternating stripes, then slice it. Sprinkle the cucumber with salt and set aside. Mix remaining ingredients to make vinegar mixture. Rinse cucumbers with cold water. Squeeze out excess water. Add to vinegar mixture.

## Okazu

When you are really hungry, you should try this dish. *Okazu* (oh-kah-zoo) is mixed vegetables and meat, usually served with rice. It makes a good meal any day of the week and uses up what is in the refrigerator. Maybe you could treat your family by cooking this for dinner. Remember to ask your parents for permission and help. This recipe serves four people.

Chris Tucker

*Young chefs at work*

½ lb.  sliced meat (beef, pork, ground beef, chicken)
½ lb.  tofu
any combination of sliced vegetables:
  green onions
  nappa (Chinese cabbage)
  mushrooms
  green beans
  green peppers

This is a very easy recipe because all you have to do is fry everything up in a frying pan and add water, a little shoyu, and sugar until you like the way it tastes. Serve okazu on rice or noodles for a tasty dinner.

## Rice

Rice is the most popular food for millions of people all over the world. The name for cooked rice is *gohan* (goh-hahn). This word also means "a full meal."

  3  cups rice
  3½  cups water

Wash and rinse the rice until the water is almost clear. Drain off all the water in the last wash. Pour in the measured amount of water. Cover and cook in a rice cooker or on the stove. Let it steam for 10 minutes after it is finished cooking. If you cook it on the stove, use a deep pan. Cook the rice at a high heat until it almost begins to boil over (the pan lid should be bouncing up and down). Lower the heat as low as possible and simmer for 15 minutes. Let the rice stand for 10 minutes and then use a wooden spoon to fluff it up.

## Spam Nigiri

If you like meat and rice, then you will like Spam *nigiri* (nee-gee-ree). It's a popular snack in Hawaii. Spam is the meat in this recipe. It tastes different and good.

  1  sheet nori (dried seaweed)
  1  cup cooked rice (see above)
     Spam (large can, cut into 12 ½-inch-long strips)

Cook Spam in frying pan (add teriyaki sauce if you like). Cut nori in half. Put a half cup of rice on each piece of nori. Spread rice out. Salt to taste. Leave 1 inch at edge of nori plain (or without rice) to seal roll. Place Spam on top of rice and roll up the nori.

*Authors making onigiri*

## Onigiri

*Onigiri* (oh-nee-gee-ree) are rice balls. Here is how you make them. First, wet your hands slightly and place a little salt on your hands. Then, scoop a handful of rice and form the rice into ovals, balls, or triangles. You can also use wood or plastic molds to form the shapes. If you want to make this look pretty, you could add seasoned seaweed or sesame seeds. Now they're ready to eat!

## Shoyu Wieners

Shoyu wieners are a delicious Japanese American food that is easy to cook. They are hot dogs cooked in soy sauce. This recipe serves five people.

5   wieners
3   tablespoons *shoyu* (soy sauce)
2   tablespoons sugar

Slice the wieners diagonally, about ¼-inch thick. Fry them in a little oil. Add shoyu and sugar. Stir until wieners are coated. Serve hot.

## Rolled Sukiyaki

*Sukiyaki* (soo-kee-yah-kee) is a great-tasting Japanese American meal made with meat and vegetables. It's easy to make and fun to eat.

½ lb.  green beans
½ lb. sukiyaki meat (thinly sliced beef)

First, boil the green beans for a very short time. Place them in a colander and drain. Cut the sukiyaki meat in half the short way. Next, place two or three string beans on the meat and roll it up. Brown the meat rolls in a skillet, turning them carefully. Pour teriyaki sauce over them.

*Slicing ingredients for rolled sukiyaki*

## Teriyaki Sauce

Teriyaki sauce is often used in Japanese American cooking. Here is how you make it:

¼  cup sugar
¼  cup soy sauce
1  teaspoon cornstarch mixed with
1  teaspoon water
Mix all ingredients together.

## Miso Shiru

*Miso shiru* (mee-soh shee-roo) may not sound good to you, but it is. This soup is good even on hot days. Miso shiru is served first at family meals, but last at formal dinners.

6  cups *dashi* (soup base)
½  lb. tofu cut into small cubes
½  cup miso paste (soybean paste)
   green onions

Put the dashi in a pan and heat it until it boils. Turn down the heat. Dissolve the miso paste in the dashi and add tofu. You can add green onions if desired. This dish serves six people who aren't too hungry.

## Udon

*Udon* (oo-dohn) noodles are big fat noodles, also called "winter noodles." You serve them hot with a udon sauce on top. Udon noodles are good in the wintertime, especially when the weather is cold. This recipe serves four people.

In a large saucepan, bring water to boil. Add noodles and stir. Bring water to a boil again, then add ½ cup cold water. Boil for 6 to 8 minutes. Test for tenderness. Remove from heat and drain. Run cold water over noodles. Before serving, pour hot water over noodles.

### *Sauce*

6  cups dashi
1  teaspoon salt
⅓  cup soy sauce
2  teaspoons sugar
2  teaspoons mirin (sweet rice wine)

In a large saucepan combine dashi, salt, shoyu, sugar, and mirin. Heat until hot, but not boiling. Remove from heat.

To serve, put noodles in bowls, pour sauce on top, then add toppings for a good flavor. Toppings: *kamaboko* (pressed fish cake), green onion, and sliced boiled eggs.

## Yaki Soba

*Yaki soba* (yah-kee soh-bah) are stir-fried noodles with meat, carrots, cabbage, or other vegetables. Yaki soba is easy to make and tastes really good. It can be served as a snack or as a meal.

| | |
|---|---|
| 1½ | tablespoons oil |
| ½ | pound of pork or beef, cut thin |
| ¼ | head of cabbage |
| 1¼ | pound package of fresh or dried yaki soba noodles |
| 4 | tablespoons *tonkatsu* sauce (seasoned sauce) |
| 1 | tablespoon soy sauce |
| 1 | carrot, cut in slivers salt and pepper |

Heat half the oil in a frying pan and sauté the meat and vegetables over medium heat for 2 to 3 minutes until tender. Season with salt and pepper. Remove from heat and set aside. Heat the remaining oil and fry noodles 3 minutes over medium heat. (If dried noodles are used, cook in boiling water until soft, then drain. Fry noodles in oil.) Add meat and vegetables. Season with tonkatsu sauce and shoyu. Fry about 2 minutes longer and serve.

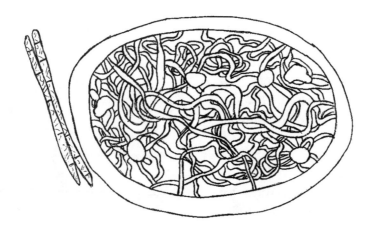

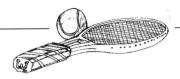

# REAL PEOPLE

*People are wonderful, people are great,*
*Happy stories, sad stories, they're all first rate.*
*We all learn from the stories of another,*
*Remember, they are someone's sister or brother.*

Japanese Americans are very proud of their heritage. Their traditions are as fascinating as the stories of their lives. We learned a lot from interviewing Japanese Americans and writing about them. For all the people we talked to, following their dream was very important. We also learned that Japanese Americans place a high value on education and the family. Even though these people followed different dreams, they are the same in many ways. They showed us their perseverance, determination, and faith.

In this section, you will read real-life stories about professors, athletes, ministers, businesspeople, and others of all ages. We felt very honored that our "real people" were willing to share their stories with us.

Many of them told us it's hard to talk about themselves, because it is not part of the Japanese American culture to discuss yourself. We think this makes their stories even more special.

## Sue Yamamoto Ando

Business was booming. "Japanese American Woman Successful Hog Raiser" flashed the headlines from local and international newspapers. The articles were about Sue Yamamoto Ando and her special achievements. In the early 1900s, there weren't many successful businesswomen, let alone Japanese American businesswomen.

Sue Yamamoto Ando was born in Utah on August 27, 1906. She was the only child born to her mother and father. When she was seven, her parents started a hog ranch. Mrs. Ando's father had a heart problem and died when she was nine, but her mother

*Sue Yamamoto Ando*

decided to keep working as a hog rancher, moving the farm to San Bernardino, California. To help out, Mrs. Ando would come home after school and get big buckets of water to fill the hogs' water troughs.

Since she had to work so hard, Mrs. Ando had a lonely life with little time for friends. The hog ranch had 300 to 400 hogs at that time. After she completed high school, she took over the ranch, because her mother couldn't handle it anymore. Although Mrs. Ando had dreams of being a doctor, she felt that taking over the ranch and helping her mother was the right thing to do.

On July 10, 1929, she married John Ando. He was attending law school when they got married. There was so much work on the ranch that he quit school to help his wife.

Mrs. Ando moved many of the hogs to Long Beach, California. She continued to run the San Bernardino ranch, as well. Mrs. Ando was so successful that she was able to get a garbage contract for more land and 25 to 30 tons of garbage each day for the hogs to eat. She bought all the hogs she could and ended up owning 6,000 hogs of her own. She kept other people's hogs on contract, too. Altogether there were nearly 14,000 hogs.

However, soon the ranch was forced to close down because of World War II. Mrs. Ando lost both ranches when she was taken to an internment camp. The land was taken over by people who divided up the ranch and sold the hogs.

Mrs. Ando has led a very hardworking life, a life worthy of respect. She appreciated her mother for teaching her to be honest and always felt that her parents were the most important people in her life. Mrs. Ando is a Nisei. She has worked hard to be treated like other Americans. When she visited Japan,

she found she wasn't accepted there, either, because she had been born in America.

Mrs. Ando thinks that Dr. Martin Luther King Jr. has helped make all people appreciate one another's heritage. She also feels that the contributions made by Japanese Americans who served in the 100th Battalion and 442nd Regimental Combat Team during World War II helped others see that they were loyal Americans.

Mrs. Ando is now 90 years old. She has two children, six grandchildren, and five great-grandchildren. She is a widow and lives with her daughter in Placentia, California.

Mrs. Ando told us she is 100 percent American. Her advice to people is, "Be a good American, but don't forget your heritage."

### George T. Sakato

George T. Sakato volunteered to fight for America. His rifle infantry unit had 9,000 Japanese Americans from all over the U.S. While Mr. Sakato and other men were fighting for their country, their families were in internment camps.

His basic training was in the marshes and on the sandy beaches of Camp Blanding, Florida. He said it rained a lot, it was always hot and muggy, and they had to sleep in the forest with snakes. Mr. Sakato was not very good with a rifle, so as soon as he was overseas, he got a machine gun.

Mr. Sakato told us about his friends in basic training and his long trip across the Atlantic Ocean. It took 28 days to reach Africa and Italy. He said his bunk on the ship was a "smelly, dark hole." The bunks were hammocks, four high and six across. Everyone

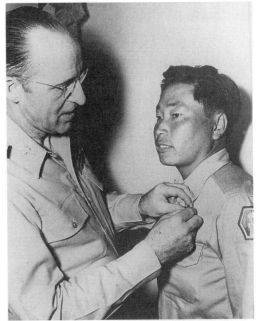

*George T. Sakato receiving the Distinguished Service Cross*

on the ship was seasick. Once when Mr. Sakato was on guard duty, the ocean was so rough that he had to tie himself to a pole so he wouldn't be washed overboard.

Finally they reached their destination near Switzerland's border. They had to march to the line of duty. The hills got steeper, and Mr. Sakato could hear machine guns firing and shells landing a mile away. While they rested, the men talked about what they would do after the war. The next thing they knew, the enemy was shooting at them. The shelling knocked Mr. Sakato 10 feet away. He was bruised and bleeding, but several of his friends were killed. This was his first experience with death.

As they moved, the soldiers had to search for minefields. Mr. Sakato would lie on his

stomach and move about 6 inches while poking his bayonet into the ground to find the mines. This was very slow. If one man made a wrong move, the mine would blow up in his face.

The men dug foxholes for shelter. Mr. Sakato said he was so scared when bullets whizzed over his head that he tried to crawl into his helmet. Soon he got better at digging foxholes. In one battle, Mr. Sakato's friends on his right and his left were hit by snipers. When the day ended, three of his friends were dead.

The platoon usually moved at night. The soldiers couldn't see anything in front of them, so each man held onto the backpack of the man in front of him. In one battle, Mr. Sakato heard gunfire and yelled at his friend Saburo Tanamachi to get down. Mr.

Tanamachi stood up anyway and was shot. Mr. Sakato couldn't stop the bleeding, and his friend died in his arms. Mr. Sakato was so angry that he jumped to his feet and ran up the hill. He yelled to the men, "Come on! We've got to take the hill!"—and they did. Mr. Sakato later found a silver dollar that Saburo always carried with him. It was made in 1921, the year that Mr. Tanamachi and Mr. Sakato were born. He took it home with him and had his friend's name engraved on it so he could always remember him. Mr. Tanamachi was awarded the Silver Star for his bravery and was one of the first Japanese Americans to be buried at Arlington National Cemetery.

There were many other battles. As the soldiers moved through the cold, wet mud, their feet turned pink and blue, and then swelled up. Mr. Sakato's feet were so cold that he took off his wet socks and put them under his armpits to warm them. Then he had to put his socks back on, even if they were still wet. He had to shove his swollen feet into his boots. The men would jokingly tell their sergeant that they needed to go home because their feet were rotting off.

One day after a battle, Mr. Sakato told his commanding officer he needed to go to the aid station because he was hurt. The commanding officer saw the bullet hole in Mr. Sakato's jacket and sent him to the aid station. At the hospital, Mr. Sakato learned that he had shrapnel in his arm and chest. The doctors left the piece of metal in his chest. They told him his body would form skin around it, and it would not move. He had to work hard to regain the movement of his arm.

While he was in the hospital, Mr. Sakato was awarded the Distinguished Service Cross for his actions with the 442nd Regimental Combat Team. He did not even know about his award until his brother told him. Mr. Sakato now attends all the reunions of World War II veterans. He is proud to have fought for his country and proud to be an American.

### Toshiko Kishimoto D'Elia

Toshiko Kishimoto D'Elia became an American citizen in March of 1957. This ceremony was a very meaningful and emotional experience for her. She cried because it meant so much to her to be free after living under a military dictatorship when she was young.

Mrs. D'Elia was born in Kyoto, Japan, on January 2, 1930. She lived with her parents, her three older brothers, and one older sister. As a child, Mrs. D'Elia enjoyed going on family outings at their favorite resort and just being with her family.

When she was unable to find a program in Japan that would train teachers of deaf children, Mrs. D'Elia came to the U.S. on a Fulbright scholarship. While she was in America, she met a man and got married without her parents' permission. After a while, she realized that her husband was not the right man for her. He loved her because she was a Japanese woman, not for the person she was inside. By that time, Mrs. D'Elia was already pregnant with Erica.

*Toshiko D'Elia running a marathon*

After her daughter was born, Mrs. D'Elia decided to go back to Japan with Erica. When she got to Japan, her parents were very angry at her for not getting permission to get married and for having a baby with a man of a different ethnic background. Mrs. D'Elia's parents said she would have to give up the baby, or she was no longer welcome at their home.

Mrs. D'Elia was very confused. She had to choose between her family and Erica. Did she want to put Erica up for adoption and stay with her family, or keep Erica and go to America? She decided to go back to America with Erica.

In America, Mrs. D'Elia worked for the New York School for the Deaf and helped

*Toshiko D'Elia with her daughter after finishing a marathon*

deaf students learn to communicate with others. One evening at a dinner party, she met a pianist, Manfred D'Elia. They married and moved to their new home in New Jersey.

One time, Mr. and Mrs. D'Elia tried to climb Mt. Rainier with friends. Mrs. D'Elia had to quit because she kept falling down, struggling, and couldn't catch her breath. The group all agreed that Mrs. D'Elia shouldn't go any farther. She was frustrated that she couldn't climb the mountain, but instead of choosing to quit, she decided to get in shape. Her friend told her to run a mile every day to increase her stamina, but she wanted to accomplish more. She wanted to be the best at whatever sport she participated in.

Once, Mrs. D'Elia found a jogging book in her daughter's gym bag. This is when Erica began to coach her mom and help her become a runner. She worked with her mom on running drills to get her in shape. In 1976, Mrs. D'Elia ran the first 26-mile

marathon in New York City. Then, in 1979, she became the oldest woman in the famous Boston Marathon to finish in less than 3 hours.

One day she got some bad news. The doctors told her that she had cancer and would have to have an operation. Mrs. D'Elia quit running and thought she might die. At that time she was reminded of one of her students named Cheryl, who stood out from the others. Cheryl had seeing and hearing handicaps along with cerebral palsy. Mrs. D'Elia felt inspired when she saw all the problems Cheryl had and how she had overcome them by teaching herself to walk. She decided that if Cheryl could do it, then so could she. So Mrs. D'Elia began training again. In the spring of 1980, she ran in the Boston Marathon again. That summer, she competed in the World Veterans Marathon Championship in Scotland. She became the first woman in the world over age 50 to run a marathon in under 3 hours.

Toshiko Kishimoto D'Elia is a strong, independent woman who has overcome cancer and other hardships in her life to accomplish her goals. She retired from teaching at the New York School for the Deaf after 36 years. We learned from her that we should always try to finish what we start. "Be true to your own convictions," she says, "and responsible to what you believe in."

### Reverend Ryo Imamura

Can you imagine what it would be like to be born in a family in which at least one son became a priest for the past 18 generations? This is the case for Reverend Ryo Imamura's family.

Rev. Imamura was born in 1944 at the Gila #2 internment camp in Arizona. He spent most of his childhood in Berkeley, California. He remembers his parents telling him he could be whatever he wanted to be. For a while he studied to be a doctor, then he was a high school math teacher. Finally, he decided to become a Buddhist priest, but his parents told him to think about it, because they wanted him to be happy with his decision. He studied at his family's temple in Fukui, Japan, and became an ordained Buddhist priest in 1972.

*Rev. Ryo Imamura (second from right)*

Rev. Imamura is proud of his heritage now, but he told us that he didn't always feel this way. He has memories of being upset by racism as a child. Ever since he was a young kid, he remembers other children making him feel that he wasn't good enough to be an American. He remembers playing the game "Bombs Over Tokyo" at recess during school and always being "bombed." He was never asked to play with the other kids after school or invited to their birthday parties. He believes other kids thought he was especially strange, because he lived right next door to the Japanese Buddhist temple, which the kids didn't understand.

When he was in the sixth grade, he was elected to be the Top Sergeant of the school traffic patrol by his class. As the Top Sergeant, he would be in charge of the older kids who helped the little ones cross the street. He was very surprised at being elected to the most important job in school, as were the schoolteachers and other grownups. They didn't expect a Japanese American kid to get this important job.

When Rev. Imamura went to school the day after election, he found out he had lost his important job. He was told he could be the Quartermaster Sergeant, instead of Top Sergeant. He was replaced by a white student. The adults told him that his voice was too soft, and this was why he couldn't be Top Sergeant. He and his parents didn't complain, even though they knew that he didn't get the job because of his race. His family knew that fighting back was not a solution, because they would not win that way. Now that he is a Buddhist priest, Rev. Imamura helps others understand that everyone should be treated fairly.

If he had to pick one person who had the biggest influence on his life, it would be his maternal grandmother, Rev. Shinobu Matsura. She was a Buddhist priest of the Jodo Shin sect and a poet. He described her as "a little chubby lady who was admired and loved by countless others around the world."

His other grandmother was also a respected figure among Buddhists and was discussed in a book about Hawaiian women.

"Continue the struggle toward wisdom and compassion," advises Rev. Imamura to young Japanese Americans. "Have pride and confidence in your unique and beautiful selves. At the same time, realize the interrelatedness of all beings and strive to bring out the best in others."

Mr. Imamura now lives in Tumwater, Washington, with his wife, Debra, and his two sons. He teaches psychology and Buddhism at Evergreen State College in Olympia, Washington. He has a master's degree in counseling and a doctorate in psychology. He was a counselor for many years and co-founded the East-West Counseling Center in Berkeley, California, which mainly helps the Asian American community. Rev. Imamura has also been active in the peace and antinuclear movement.

We wonder if one of the Reverend's sons will have the desire to become a Buddhist priest like his father. He would be the 19th generation—more than 500 years of Buddhist priests in one family!

### Dr. Lane Hirabayashi

Dr. Lane Hirabayashi has some good advice for young kids. "Learning about your heritage is very important," says the associate professor of anthropology and Asian American Studies at the University of Colorado. "This helps you appreciate all the things your family did for you. This will give you courage and strength."

Dr. Hirabayashi was born on October 17, 1952, in Seattle, Washington. He is Sansei, or third generation. His mom is Norwegian and his father is Japanese. This makes him and his younger sister, Jan, half–Japanese American. Dr. Hirabayashi grew up in Mill Valley, California. It took his parents a long time to find a place to live where there were good schools,

*Dr. Lane Hirabayashi*

because many people wouldn't rent houses to Japanese people in the 1950s.

When he was growing up, his parents thought it was important to be good and never to lie or steal. They also believed in the Golden Rule—"Do unto others as you would have them do unto you." They thought education and helping others were necessary, too. Dr. Hirabayashi told us he was happy his mom shared her love of books and learning with her children.

In the fourth grade, one kid in Dr. Hirabayashi's art class teased him and made fun of his last name. That really upset him. He walked outside, sat on the swings, and felt bad. Later, the art teacher told him that she liked his last name, and that made him feel better.

Dr. Hirabayashi's heroes changed as he grew up. When he was little, he looked up to the older kids in the neighborhood. When he was in junior high and high school, he liked the musicians James Brown and the Beatles. During this time, he wanted to be a musician and played in some blues bands in the San Francisco Bay area.

In college, his heroes were his dad, uncle, and grandfather, Shungo John Hirabayashi. He remembers his father and uncle telling him about their hard times. In 1922, Shungo John Hirabayashi's land was taken away by the U.S. government, because he wasn't allowed to become an American citizen. The family didn't think that was legal, so they went to court to get their land back. The court people felt it *was* the right thing to do, so the Hirabayashi family never got their land back.

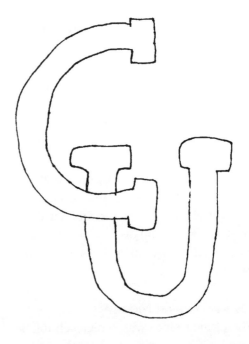

During World War II, his uncle Gordon Hirabayashi, who was a Quaker, didn't think it was right or fair that the Japanese Americans had to go into internment camps, so he refused to go. He decided to go to court about it. The Quakers helped him by raising money and supporting his beliefs. When he went to court, the judge didn't agree with him, so he was sent to jail in Arizona. They wouldn't pay for the trip, and they didn't care how he got there, so he hitchhiked from Washington all the way to Arizona to go to jail! He showed he was honest by getting himself to the jail. Dr. Hirabayashi admired both his grandfather and his uncle, because they struggled for equal rights and never gave up.

Even though he was a terrible student in high school, Dr. Hirabayashi made up for it in college. After high school, he earned his

B.A., M.A., and Ph.D. degrees. Besides teaching at a university, he's also part of a program that teaches classes and does research about different racial minorities in the U.S. He married his wife, Marilyn, in 1988, and has a stepdaughter, Denise. He believes his family and his work are the most important parts of his life.

"By getting the best education that you can and by taking school seriously," Dr. Hirabayashi told us, "you can find out about the world while you discover what you're really good at." We think that's a great lesson to remember!

## Reverend David Nieda

When David Nieda was in high school, he went on a silent retreat one day. He was sitting quietly under a tree, when he felt God trying to call him. Did God want him to be a minister? David decided not to answer the call, because he wanted to go to college and make lots of money.

Rev. Nieda attended college at the University of California at Los Angeles (UCLA). His desire to make money gave him many ideas of what he would like to do. Would he be a lawyer, businessman, disc jockey, newspaper reporter, or teacher? He was getting close to graduation, but he still didn't know what he should do.

Once again, he felt God trying to call him. This time Rev. Nieda answered the call and decided to become a minister. He went to the Iliff School of Theology in Denver, Colorado, where he started working with the youth group at a Methodist church. He knew this was important for

*Rev. David Nieda*

him, because he could achieve his goal of helping Japanese American youth develop pride in their heritage and learn more about God.

Rev. Nieda works hard every year bringing pride and the love of God to Asian Camp, where he teaches in the summer. It's a summer camp sponsored by Asian American Methodist churches from the Pacific Northwest, California, and Colorado. He told us that students in grade seven through college spend the week learning about what it means to be Asian American. He also shows them that scripture can be vital to their personal lives. They learn about racism and injustice around the world. They also may participate in a sharing show or even a mini dance competition.

Rev. Nieda is a Nisei Japanese American. Most Nisei ministers are in their 50s and 60s, but Rev. Nieda is young. He was born on January 27, 1964. We think his young age helps him relate to the youth in his church.

If he could change one thing in our country, Rev. Nieda would want fairness and justice for everyone in our society. If this happened, there would be less racism and more friendship between people of all races.

The most important things in Rev. Nieda's life are his ministry and his identity as a Japanese American. His advice to Japanese American youth is to be curious about your heritage and to have a friendship with God, who wants you to be proud of who you are.

## Garrett Ito

"If I were magic," says Garrett Ito, "I would make people more caring and loving toward one another and towards themselves. This is my wish for the world."

While many 29-year-olds are busy partying and having a good time, Mr. Ito is also having a good time, but in a different way. The most important thing in his life is serving others. He wants to make our world a better place to live by serving his family, community, and friends. Mr. Ito thinks he can affect people the most by developing his own talents and sharing them. This feeling led to one of the most important decisions of his life—going to graduate school. He's studying all sorts of things about the Earth, because he wants to be a geophysicist. A geophysicist is a scientist who studies what the Earth is made of and how it's changing. Right now, he is working on his Ph.D. at the Massachusetts Institute of Technology (MIT) in Cambridge, Massachusetts.

Mr. Ito has lots of heroes. We think this is because he looks for the good in everyone he meets. His first hero was Steve Austin, the main character on *The Six Million Dollar Man* television show. Now his hero is Greg LeMond, a famous bicycle racer. He likes riding bikes himself, and he respects Greg for all the races he has won.

Born on March 4, 1967, Mr. Ito and his family moved to Anaheim, California, where he lived until he was 13. After that, they

*Garrett Ito*

moved to Englewood, Colorado, where he lived until he went to college. In addition to his mom and dad, he also has a younger sister, Ellyn. When he was little, his parents thought that developing self-esteem, being a hard worker, and having personal values were all important. This made him want to grow up and make a difference in the world.

When he was growing up, his family celebrated holidays, especially New Year's Day. Sometimes, in the summer, his mother and sister would dance in the Obon. This is a summer festival where Japanese Americans get together to dance folk dances in celebration of their ancestors. Everyone dresses in traditional summer kimonos called yukata.

Being Japanese American is something that Mr. Ito is very proud of. When he was a senior in college, he visited Japan and had a wonderful time! He learned a lot about his grandparents and came to understand and respect their values. He appreciates his Japanese heritage and thinks that

being different makes you special. That's what he thinks is great about America—everyone has a unique heritage.

## Kimberly Po

Have you ever heard of Kimberly Po? If you haven't, you should know that she's a touring tennis professional. Miss Po lives in Westwood, California, near the UCLA campus. She was born on October 20, 1971, and she's half-Chinese and half-Japanese.

As Ms. Po grew up, she did a lot of things with her older brother, Greg, such as going to the park and playing games and sports. Her parents thought that she should treat others as she would like to be treated. As a child, her family celebrated

*Kimberly Po practicing tennis*

Japanese and Chinese New Years as well as other holidays.

Miss Po played competitive soccer before she discovered tennis. Although she enjoyed soccer very much, she sometimes got frustrated that some of the players weren't trying as hard as she was. At 9 years of age, she decided to give tennis a try. By the age of 11, she was playing in national tournaments, and she's been playing ever since.

Miss Po became really good at tennis when she was in high school. In 1987, when she was 16, she ranked #3 for singles and #1 for doubles nationally in her age group. She was also in honors classes in her school. As you can see, she's not only good at tennis, she's good at a lot of other things, too.

Miss Po is glad we're writing this book to fight racism. She has had to face this problem herself. One day, while she was in high school, she was walking to her car when she saw two boys looking at her and making fun of her eyes. When she saw them, she wanted to go up to them and tell their mother what the two boys had

just done, but she didn't. Miss Po was shocked, because she thought racism was all gone, but it wasn't—and still isn't.

In 1989, Miss Po went to college at UCLA for 2 years before she decided to play tennis professionally. It was a hard decision for her, because both tennis and education are meaningful to her. She wants to play tennis for 6 or 7 more years and then retire from tennis, go back to college, and graduate. Then she wants to go to law school to study environmental law.

Miss Po thinks people should be more aware of other people's different backgrounds and respect them. She also thinks it's important to learn about your own heritage and know what your parents and grandparents and great-grandparents did, so you don't have to go through what they did.

Being both Japanese American and Chinese American has made Kimberly Po more aware of all the other races in the world around her.

## Jill Ogawa

Have you ever been teased or bullied? What did you do? What did you say in response? When Jill Ogawa was in high school, she had to decide how to handle such a situation.

Ms. Ogawa was about to serve the ball in a high school volleyball tournament, when some fans from the other school started shouting at her. They called her "Jap" and "samurai." She had to decide whether to take a stand or to continue playing. She decided to stop the game

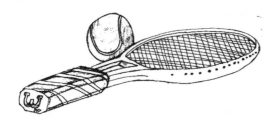

and ask the referee to remove the fans. She was very nervous.

At first the referee laughed, and Ms. Ogawa had to tell her again. Finally, the fans were told to stop, but they were not asked to leave. Ms. Ogawa wondered if she did the right thing by interrupting the game. Later, she decided it had been the right thing to do, because the fans were wrong for saying what they did. Ms. Ogawa told us that the important thing to remember is not to ignore racial remarks or prejudice. Stand up for what you believe.

Ms. Ogawa was born on September 22, 1972. She is now in college and wants to be a doctor. As a child, she was very active. She lived near many boys and played sports with them all the time. When she was 3 years old, she started taking gymnastics lessons. This was when her parents first realized that she might be a good athlete someday.

She played sports throughout her teenage years. When she was in high school, she played on varsity volleyball,

*Jill Ogawa, lacrosse player*

basketball, and lacrosse teams. She won many awards, including a Most Valuable Player award in volleyball and lacrosse, and an honorable mention for all-American lacrosse. She was captain of her volleyball and lacrosse teams.

People sometimes wonder if they can be good at sports if they are short, but Ms. Ogawa has proved you can be. She has a good sense of humor about her height. She says she's "five feet tall on a good day." Her coaches thought she would have problems competing against taller players, but she believes hard work helped her succeed.

Jill Ogawa says that going to college gives her more opportunities to have a career. She knows that her education is more important than her participation in sports. She was on the honor roll all through high school and is now on the merit list at Kenyon College in Ohio.

Ms. Ogawa goes to a Methodist church where most of the members are Japanese Americans. She practices her Christian faith and many Japanese cultural things, like origami and Japanese dances.

For many years, Ms. Ogawa has gone to a Methodist Asian American summer camp. She likes participating in the camp because it's a place where race doesn't matter, and a person is accepted because of who she is. At camp, the kids become good friends with other Christians and learn how to handle prejudice. Ms. Ogawa has learned how important it is to feel good about yourself. She thinks young people should learn about their own culture and the other cultures in America.

# OUR VISION FOR A BETTER TOMORROW

As we were writing and working on this book, one of the important things we learned was about the harm of stereotyping. Stereotyping is when you look at someone and think you know them just by their race or outside appearance. Sometimes stereotypes fit, but usually they don't. If you think you know a person just by looking at them, you're probably wrong. You have to get to know them by talking and playing with them.

Here are some things we, the Japanese Americans in the workshop, wrote to show that we are "real people," too.

I am Japanese American. Something about me I want you to know is . . .

. . . I would like to live in the mountains and have a big house with a lot of land and two horses.

. . . I like to dance. When I dance I can let go of all the stress I have collected during the day.

. . . I don't speak much Japanese, and I don't know a lot about Japan.

. . . I feel good about being myself because, though I'm different in many ways, I'm like other people, too.

. . . I'm always glad to learn more about my culture.

. . . My favorite subject in school is reading, and I like to read about many different things.

Chris Tucker

*Young authors taking a break*

Chris Tucker

*Sharing lunch with friends*

. . . I am good in math.

. . . I love art.

. . . I feel hurt when I get made fun of at school because I'm Japanese American. People shouldn't make fun of me just because I'm different.

. . . I like the Japanese American values of respecting other people, enjoying the arts, and thinking that school is one of the most important things in life.

. . . I'm good at judo. I took first place at the Junior Olympics in Michigan.

. . . My favorite food is Mexican food, especially cheese enchiladas.

. . . My favorite food is pizza.

. . . I eat more American food than Japanese food.

. . . I am glad that I am Japanese American, but I don't like it when people make fun of our food, our culture, or me.

. . . I like basketball. My favorite teams are the Bulls, Magic, Lakers, and Hornets.

. . . My hobbies are collecting comic books and CDs.

. . . I'm having fun learning about my heritage and ancestry.

. . . I like it when my grandpa tells me about when he lived in Japan.

. . . I'm 12 years old. I have samurai on both sides of my family. My grandpa went to an internment camp and my grandma had to move to Colorado.

. . . I feel hurt when I hear about the awful discrimination that my grandparents, parents, and other relatives endured.

. . . I wish others would judge me like anyone else. I think that it is really unfair to judge people by how they look and their ethnic background.

. . . I want people to know that Japanese Americans are Americans, not Japanese. They are born in America.

. . . I am half African American. I didn't know much about my Japanese American heritage, but I am learning a lot about it with this book.

. . . I am Buddhist. I am Yonsei, or fourth generation. On my dad's side, I am part Irish and Swedish.

. . . I don't like people to call me "Jap."

. . . I can play taiko drums and do origami, and I go to the Denver Buddhist Temple every Sunday. I used to be one of the only Asian people in my school, but more are beginning to come.

. . . I can write some of the Japanese alphabet, and I can read and speak a little bit of the Japanese language.

. . . I want to learn more about my heritage now.

. . I am extremely proud to be a Japanese American!

Here are some of the things that we, the non–Japanese American authors, learned while writing this book:

. . . Japanese Americans have faced tough times, like during wartime. The government thought that the Japanese Americans were spies, and people said mean things to them.

. . . Japanese Americans were taken away from their homes and put into internment camps.

. . . When you see someone who's different because they're handicapped, or they're from a different heritage, or they have problems, treat them the same as you would treat your best friend.

. . . Japanese Americans have been very loyal to their country. Even while their parents were put in internment camps, their sons fought for the United States in World War II.

. . . I learned about the different generations of Japanese Americans.

. . . Japanese really like to have their food look good.

. . . Americans come in all different kinds and love their country very much.

. . . Many people are treated very badly. If we try hard, we can change the way we treat one another.

. . . Japanese Americans are just like everybody else.

# WESTRIDGE YOUNG WRITERS WORKSHOP PARTICIPANTS

*The authors*

*The authors*

## STUDENT AUTHORS

Zachery Arnone
Justin D. Boehm
James V. Boutwell
Shannon C. Boutwell
Zachary A. Brown
Alyssa Kelly Burnell
Kimberly Lynn Burnell
Jon Isao Campbell
Nicholas Kiyoshi Campbell
Scott S. Chikuma
Holly Kay Clark
Jesse Cowand
Nichole I. Cox
Tara Liana Dell
Dustin DeWitt
Dara Reiko Domoto
Drew Tsutomu Domoto
Isaac Edwards
Kevin Everson
Connarty M. Fagan
Jared J. Fukunaga
Lindsay A. Fukunaga
Jessica Erin Funk
Bryce Soichi Fushimi
Kathryn Goto

Desiree Hatsumi Fushimi
Keegan Yoichi Fushimi
Dan Gorton
Christopher R. Hale
Becky K. Hamada
Sarah Louise Heinrich
Tomiko Cim Herder
Christopher Shigeo Holland
Kimberly Akiko Horiuchi
Geoffrey Hikaru Ida
Kenji Kamibayashi
Kimiko Sara Kano
Matthew Kazuo Kawakami
Andrea C. Kelly
Thomas Payton Knight
Heather Anne Krohn
Andrea Nicole Lowe
Kristin MacCary
Michael Manning
José A. Martinez III
Ray Christopher Maruyama
Skye Akiko Masaki
Akiko Miyake-Stoner
Mary Agnes Moore
Austin LaMar Mori
Mario Yuzo Nieto
Amber Kikuye Noguchi

Akihiro Kevin Okamoto
Larry Ray Ornelas
Patricia R. Ornelas
Sandra Marie Ornelas
Janine R. Ota
Courtney Akemi Ozaki
Keiko Ann Ozaki
Margaret Tamiko Ozaki
Shannon Masako Ozaki
Neha Pall
Jeremy C. Patterson
Joey L. Pettit
Josh J. Pettit
Jackie Pilling
Deborah Lynne Rhodes
Jessie Rickard
Alexi Rothschild
Zachary Rothschild
Kathryn Morishige Rowen
Harold Sampson Jr.
Leslie Akimi Sasa
Cathryn M. Shibata
Robert P. Shibata
Chance Matthew Siegele
Chase Michael Siegele
Dirk James Sisneros
Drew Thomas Sisneros

Stefanie Southall
Erika Sullivan
Joseph Mark Suyeishi
Fumi Takase
Janel Lynette Uyeda
Courtney Nicole Ward
Brandon Weaver
Jared Wertz
Nicole Wessels
Melissa Michiko Whittall
Joloni Shane Williams
Andrew Thomas Wong
Jason Michael Wong
Allison Keiko Wong
Jennifer Aiko Wong

*The high school mentors*

*The teachers* (sensei)

## TEACHERS

Annette M. Acevedo-Martinez
Roxanne Carlson Boat
Janice Sayo Campbell
Lisa Caricato
Sue Chichester
Patricia Hagerty Coats
Judith H. Cozzens, Director
Michelle Michiko Crocket
Sandie Dell
Nancy Domoto
Eddie Katsumoto Ellington
Jane Fujioka
Sandy Fukunaga
Mary Ann Garcia-Pettit
Jo-Anne Ginther
Lorraine Gutierrez
Brenda F. Hale

Yoshiye Hamada
Helen Cozzens Healy,
    Co-Director
Jane Hilbert
Donna Inouye Holland
Peggy Imatani
Diane Iwersen
Robbin Kitashima
Melissa R. Lobach
Trudy Ogawa
Judy Natsuko Okamoto
Annetta Ornelas
Amy S. Pound, Co-Director
Pat Rhodes
Carolyn Takeshita
Katy Tobo
Sandy Tsubokawa Whittall
Bobbi Shinto Wong

## MENTORS

These high school and college
mentors assisted the writing program and helped in many ways.


Kirsten Frederiksen-Cherry
Shelly Fujikawa
Kiku Lyn Herder
Beth Hitztaler
Aaron Horiuchi
Claire Imatani
Emily Imatani
Jon Kusumi
Kim Lantz
Ryan Lantz
Keith Masaki
Lukas Hideo Mori
David Namura
Paul Namura
Natal Newhouse
Lisa Okamoto
Stuart Ota
Kim Wada
Jennnifer Wanifuchi
Zeni Whittall
Tonia Young

# GLOSSARY OF JAPANESE WORDS

*ahiru* (ah-hee-roo)—duck

*bachi* (bah-chee)—sticks used to play taiko and samisen

*Bodhidharma* (boh-dee-dar-mah)—a Zen priest who took his teachings to China

*Bon* (bohn), also *Obon* (oh-bohn)—a Buddhist festival to welcome spirits of the dead

*Bon-Odori* (bohn oh-doh-ree)—an Obon dance

*bonen kai* (boh-nehn kye)—a year-end party

*bonsai* (bohn-sigh)—the art of raising miniature plants and trees with unusually shaped branches

*buta* (boo-tah)—pig

*daikon* (dy-kohn)—radish

*dans* (dahns)—steps in the black-belt rank

*dana* (dah-nah)—selfless giving

*daruma* (dah-roo-mah)—an egg-shaped doll-like Japanese figure

*dashi* (dah-shee)—a soup base

*do itashimashite* (doh ee-tah-shee-mahsh-teh)—you're welcome

*dojo* (doh-joh)—a martial arts school

*domo arigato gozaimasu* (doh-moh ah-ree-gah-toh goh-zah-ee-mahs)—thank you

*furoshiki* (foo-roh-shee-kee)—a scarf with a Japanese design

*futon* (foo-tohn)—a type of bed

*gaman* (gah-mahn)—tough it out

*genki desu* (gehn-kee dehs)—I'm fine

*genki desu ka* (gehn-kee dehs-ka)—how are you?

*geta* (geh-tah)—Japanese wooden sandals

*gi* (gee, with a hard "g")—a white uniform worn to do martial arts

*giri* (gee-ree)—obligation

*Go* (goh)—a Japanese board game

*go* (goh)—five

*gohan* (goh-hahn)—cooked rice, a full meal

*gomen nasai* (goh-mehn nah-sigh)—I'm sorry

*Gosei* (goh-say)—fifth generation

*hachi* (hah-chee)—eight

*hachimaki* (hah-chee-mah-kee)—a headband

*Hachisei* (hah-chee-say)—eighth generation

*haiku* (hy-koo)—a 17-syllable poem

*happi* (hah-pee)—a kimono coat

*Harugakita* (hah-roo-gah-kee-tah)—a name of a dance and song

*hashi* (hah-shee)—chopsticks

*Hashi Kyoso* (hah-shee kyoh-soh)—a Japanese game played with chopsticks

*Hassei* (hah-say)—eighth generation

*hina-dan* (hee-nah dahn)—a doll stand

*Hina Matsuri* (hee-nah mah-tsoo-ree)—annual Girls' Day or Doll Festival

*Hina Ningyo* (hee-nah neen-gyoh)—miniature dolls that represent the Imperial Court of Japan 300 years ago

*hiragana* (hee-rah-gah-nah)—a type of Japanese writing for everyday use

*hitsuji* (hee-tsoo-jee)—sheep

*Hon dashi* (hohn dah-shee)—a concentrated soup base

*ichi* (ee-chee)—one

*ikebana* (ee-keh-dah-nah)—the art of flower arranging

*ikimasho* (ee-kee-mah-shoh)—let's go

*ikkyu* (ee-kyoo)—the first level in judo

*inu* (ee-noo)—dog

*Issei* (ees-say)—first generation

*Jan Ken Po* (jahn kehn poh)—a Japanese American game similar to "rock, scissors, paper"

*ju* (joo)—ten

*judo* (joo-doh)—a type of martial art, means "the gentle way"

*Jusei* (joo-say)—tenth generation

*kachi-kachis* (kah-chee kah-chees)—wooden instruments clicked between two fingers like castanets

*kaeru* (kah-eh-roo)—frog

*kamaboko* (kah-mah-bok-koh)—pressed fish cake

*kanashi* (kah-nah-shee)—I'm sad

*kanji* (kan-jee)—a type of Japanese formal writing

*kansha* (kahn-shah)—gratitude toward parents and ancestors

*karaoke* (kah-rah-oh-keh)—singing on stage along with a tape

*karate* (kah-rah-teh)—a type of martial art

*kata* (kah-tah)—several offensive and defensive movements in karate

*katakana* (kah-tah-kah-nah)—a type of Japanese writing used for words that are not originally Japanese

*ken* (kehn)—a Japanese prefecture

*kendo* (kehn-doh)—Japanese fencing, a type of martial art

*kenjinkai* (kehn-jeen-kye)—a group for people from the same ken

*kibi dango* (kee-bee dahn-goh)—rice dumplings

*kimono* (kee-mohn-noh)—a long robe, means "the thing worn"

*kombu* (kohm-boo)—seaweed used in cooking

*konban wa* (kohn-bahn wah)—good evening

*konnichi wa* (kohn-nee-chee wah)—good day

*koto* (koh-toh)—a plucked string instrment

*ku* (koo)—nine

*kuro mame* (koo-roh mah-meh)—black beans

*Kyoto* (kyoh-toh)—a city in Japan

*Kyusei* (kyoo-say)—ninth generation

*mirin* (mee-reen)—Japanese sweet rice wine used for cooking

*miso* (mee-soh)—soybean paste

*miso shiru* (mee-soh shee-roo)—a kind of soup

*mochi tsuki* (moh-chee tsoo-kee)—sweet rice ball

*Moribana* (moh-ree-bah-nah)—a style of ikebana

*mukashi banashi* (moo-kah-shee bah-nah-shee)—Japanese folk tales

*Nageire* (nah-geh-ee-reh)—a style of ikebana

*Nage no Kata* (nah-geh noh kah-tah)—a set of 15 different throws in judo

*naginata* (nah-gee-nah-tah)—a martial art

*Nanasei* (nah-nah-say)—seventh generation

*nappa* (nah-pah)—Chinese cabbage

*neko* (neh-koh)—cat

*nezumi* (neh-zoo-mee)—mouse

*ni* (nee)—two

*Nihongakko* (nee-hohn-gah-koh)—Japanese language school

*nikkyu* (nee-kyoo)— second level in judo

*Nisei* (nee-say)—second generation

*nishime* (nee-shee-meh)—a vegetable dish

*nori* (noh-ree)—dried seaweed

*obento* (oh-behn-toh)—a packed lunch in a special lunch box

*obi* (oh-bee)—a sash worn with a kimono

*Obon* (oh-bohn), also *Bon* (bohn)—a Buddhist festival to welcome spirits of the dead

*ohayo gozaimasu* (oh-hah-yo goh-zah-ee-mahs)—good morning

*okazu* (oh-kah-zoo)—mixed vegetables and meat

*ondori* (ohn-doh-ree)—rooster

*onigiri* (oh-nee-gee-ree)—rice balls

*origami* (oh-ree-gah-mee)—the art of paper folding

*Oshogatsu* (oh-shoh-gah-tsoo)—New Year's Day

*oyasumi nasai* (o-yah-soo-mee nah-sye)—good night

*ozoni* (oh-zoh-nee)—a type of soup

*Rikka* (ree-kah)—a style of ikebana

*roku* (ro-koo)—six

*Rokusei* (roh-koo-say)—sixth generation

*sachiko* (sah-chee-koh)—happiness

*sake* (sah-keh)—rice wine

*sakura* (sah-koo-rah)—cherry blossoms

*samisen* (sah-mee-sehn)—traditional Japanese stringed instrument similar to a banjo

*samurai* (sah-moo-rye)—warrior

*san* (sahn)—three

*sankyu* (sahn-kyoo)—the third level in judo

*Sansei* (sahn-say)—third generation

*sashimi* (sah-shee-mee)—raw fish

*sayonara* (sah-yoh-nah-rah)—good-bye

*sei* (say)—generation or an age

*sensei* (sehn-say)—teacher

*shakuhachi* (shah-koo-hah-chee)—an instrument made of bamboo, with finger holes, like a flute

*shi* (shee)—four

*shichi* (shee-chee)—seven

*shiro* (shee-roh)—white

*shodo* (shoh-doh)—Japanese calligraphy

*shoji* (shoh-jee)—sliding doors with white squares of paper in them

*Shoka* (shoh-kah)—a style of ikebana

*shoyu* (shoh-yoo)—soy sauce

*sukoshi* (soo-koh-shee)—a little bit

*soba* (soh-bah)—brown noodles made from buckwheat

*somen* (soh-men)—summer noodles made from wheat flour

*sukiyaki* (soo-kee-yah-kee)—meal of meat and vegetables

*sumi* (soo-mee)—an ink stick used in sumi-e

*sumi-e* (soo-mee-eh)—the art of ink painting

*sunomono* (soo-noh-moh-noh)—cucumber salad

*tabi* (tah-bee)—a type of Japanese sock worn with a kimono

*taiko* (ty-koh)—an ancient form of drumming

*tako* (tah-koh)—kite, also means octopus

*Tango No Sekku* (tahn-goh noh seh-koo)—Boys' Day

*Tanko Bushi* (tahn-koh boo-shee)—a folk dance

*tatami* (tah-tah-mee)—a mat

*tempura* (tehm-poo-rah)—deep-fried vegetables or seafood

*tengu* (tehn-goo)—goblin children

*tofu* (toh-foo)—soybean curd

*tonkatsu* (tohn-kah-tsoo)—seasoned sauce

*tori* (toh-ree)—bird

*torii* (toh-ree-ee)—a wooden gateway with two columns and a crossbar on top

*tsukemono* (tsoo-keh-moh-noh)—pickled vegetables

*udon* (oo-dohn)—winter noodles made from wheat flour

*ureshii* (oo-reh-shee-ee)—I'm happy

*ushi* (oo-shee)—cow

*yaki soba* (yah-kee soh-bah)—stir-fried noodles with meat and vegetables

*Yonsei* (yohn-say)—fourth generation

*yukata* (yoo-kah-tah)—summer cotton kimonos

*zori* (zoh-ree)—thongs

# CALENDAR

Japanese Americans celebrate the same holidays as other Americans, but they also might celebrate many holidays, celebrations, and festivals from their heritage country, Japan. Using the information in the Calendar, you can find out other dates that are important to the Japanese American community.

## January

**New Year's Day**, December 31 to January 3—Celebration of the passing of one year and the arrival of the next. This holiday is called *O-shogatsu* in Japanese.

**New Year's Festival** in Moiliili (Hawaii)—A 2-day event highlighting New Year's customs and traditions as they are practiced in Hawaii and Japan. For more information, contact the Japanese Cultural Center of Hawaii and the Moiliili Community Center, 2454 South Beretania Street, Honolulu, HI 96826; (808) 945-7633. Call for exact date and time.

**Japanese New Year Celebration** (Massachusetts)—The Children's Museum, 300 Congress Street, Boston, MA 02210-1034; (617) 426-6500. Admission free with museum entrance fee. Call for exact date and time.

## February

**Cherry Blossom Festival**: Culture and Craft Fair (Hawaii)—A variety of children's games and activities in celebration of this Japanese event which takes place between January and April nationwide. Contact Honolulu Japanese Junior Chamber of Commerce, 2454 South Berretania Street, #205, Honolulu, HI 96826; (808) 949-2255.

**Hatsume Fair** (Florida)—Celebration of the coming of spring. Morikami Museum, 4000

Morikami Park Road, Delray Beach, FL 33446; (407) 495-0233. Call for exact date and time.

**Sakura Festival** (Alabama)—Japanese games, art workshops, calligraphy, and stage shows. Takes place through April. Contact University of Alabama, Japan Program, Box 870254, Tuscaloosa, AL 35487-0254; (205) 348-5312.

## March

**Doll Festival**, March 3, (Nationwide)—Families celebrate their daughters. Sets of dolls representing ancient imperial court are displayed. In Japanese, this festival is called *Hina Matsuri*. Please check with your local Japanese American organization for events in your area.

—Colorado, early March. Contact: Simpson United Methodist Church, 6001 Wolff, Arvada, CO 80003; (303) 428-7963

**National Cherry Blossom Festival** (Washington, D.C.)—A 6-day festival in celebration of the friendship between the U.S. and Japan. Occurs whenever the cherry trees along the Potomac River bloom, usually between March 20 and April 15. Arts and crafts show, parade, and more. Contact: National Cherry Blossom Festival, P.O. Box 77312, Washington, D.C., 20013; (202) 547-1500.

**Smithsonian Kite Festival** (Washington, D.C.)—Annual handmade kite-flying competition. Prizes awarded in many categories, including rokakku, Japanese-style, six-sided kites. Contact: The Smithsonian Associates, 1100 Jefferson Drive, Rm. 3077, S.W., Washington, D.C. 20560; (202) 357-3030.

## April

**Cherry Blossom Festival** (Washington)—Includes Japanese culture and customs and a parade in Japantown. Contact: Japan Center, 1520 Webster Street, San Francisco, CA 94115; (415) 922-6776. Or contact Seattle Cherry Blossom and Culture Festival, P.O. Box 9055, Seattle, WA 98109; (206) 622-7281.

## May

**Asian Pacific Heritage Month** (Nationwide)—Held nationally in honor of Asian Pacific Americans since 1979.

**Children's Day**, May 5 (Nationwide)—The beginning of summer according to the lunar calendar, and a day to celebrate children's future. This day is called *Tango No Sekku* in Japanese. For more information, contact: Japanese American Cultural and Community Center, 244 S. San Pedro, Suite 505, Los Angeles, CA 90012; (213) 628-2725

beginning of summer according to the lunar calendar, and a day to celebrate children's future. This day is called *Tango No Sekku* in Japanese. For more information, contact: Japanese American Cultural and Community Center, 244 S. San Pedro, Suite 505, Los Angeles, CA 90012; (213) 628-2725

**Discover Children's Day: An Art Festival** (Hawaii)—Statewide art contest for ages 5 to 12 to depict what Children's Day means to them. Contact: Japanese Cultural Center of Hawaii, 2454 South Berretania Street, Honolulu, HI 96826; (808) 945-7633.

**Hina Matsuri** (Nationwide)—A weekend festival honoring the Buddha's birthday. Contact your local Buddhist Temple.

   —In California, Japanese Village, Plaza, 800, West 6th Street, Suite 600, Los Angeles, CA 90017; (213) 683-0500. Call for date and time.

## June

**Festival of American Folklife** (Washington, D.C.)—Celebrates the variety of different cultures in the United States. Held at the National Mall, Washington, D.C. Contact: Convention and Visitor's Association, 1212 New York Avenue, 6th Floor, N.W., Washington, D.C. 20005; (202) 789-7000. Held last weekend in June and first weekend of July.

## July

**"Festival of Lanterns"** or **Bon Odori** (Illinois)—Outdoor dances to the music of different regions of Japan. Contact Midwest Buddhist Temple,

435 West Menomonee Street, Chicago, IL 60614; (312) 943-7801.

**Obon Festival** (Nationwide)—Held on the Second Saturday in July. Obon-dori dancing in full costume to authentic Japanese folk music. Contact a local Buddhist Temple for celebrations in your area.

   —Fresno Buddhist Church, 1340 Kern Street, Fresno, CA 93706; (209) 442-4054.

   —Salt Lake City Buddhist Church, 211 West First Street South, Salt Lake City, Utah 84101; (209) 442-4054.

   —Buddhist National Headquarters, 1910 Octavia Street, San Francisco, CA 94109; (415) 776-5600.

## August

**Ginza Holiday: Japanese Cultural Festival** (Illinois)—Master craftsmen from Tokyo demonstrate their arts, Japanese folk music and classical dancing, martial arts, taiko (drums), ikebana (flower arrangements), and cultural displays. For more information, contact Midwest Buddhist Temple, 435 W. Menomonee Street, Chicago, IL 60614; (312) 943-7801.

**Nihonmachi Street Fair** (California)—A well-known street fair held every year at the Japan Center in San Francisco. Contact Nihonmachi Fair Committee, 1840 Center Street, San Francisco, CA 94115; (415) 392-4520.

**Nisei Week** (California)—A 9-day celebration that includes cultural exhibits, karate and judo demonstrations, sword tournaments, and dancing. For more information, contact Nisei Week Committee (213) 687-7193.

We didn't find any important events for Japanese Americans between September and December. To find out about other significant dates for Japanese Americans, use the Resource Guide on page 145.

# RESOURCE GUIDE

Here is a partial list of Japanese American-related organizations that might be of use to you. To find out more information about Japanese American groups and activities in your area, contact one of them. Dates, times, and admission prices change often, so please call ahead.

## Alabama

**The Children's Hands-On Museum**, 2213 University Boulevard, Tuscaloosa, AL 35403; (205) 349-4235. Permanent Japan House exhibit.

## Alaska

**Japanese Heritage Club**, 523 Jordt Circle, Anchorage, AK 99504; (907) 243-0600. Seeks to sustain the cultural heritage of Japanese Americans in the Anchorage area.

## California

**Asian American Curriculum Project (AACP)**, 234 Main Street, San Mateo, CA 94401; (415) 343-9408 or (800) 874-2242. Develops and promotes Asian-American studies and curriculum material to schools, libraries, and Asian Americans. Publishes the annual Asian American Curriculum Project—Catalogue.

**Berkeley Art Center**, 1275 Walnut Street, Berkeley, CA 94709; (510) 644-6893. Museum activities include an exhibit called "Asian Roots, Western Soil: Japanese influences in American Culture." Annual Youth Arts Festival in March. Open Thursday to Sunday, 12 p.m.–5 p.m. Admission is free. Membership: $20 for students, $25 for adults, $35 for families.

**Craft & Folk Art Museum**, 5800 Wilshire Boulevard, Los Angeles, CA 90036; (213) 937-5544. Includes a collection of Japanese and Japanese American folk art, and sponsors annual programs such as the "Festival of the Masks."

Open Tuesday to Sunday, 11 a.m.–5 p.m. Free for children under 12; $2.50 for students; $4 for adults.

**Japan Center**, Post and Buchanan Streets, Japantown, San Francisco, CA 94115; (415) 922-6776. Peace Pagoda, shops, restaurants, Japanese Bathhouse. Open Monday to Friday, 10 a.m.–10 p.m.; Saturday to Sunday, 9 a.m.–10 p.m. Admission is free.

**The Japanese American Cultural and Community Center (JACCC)**, 244 South San Pedro Street, Los Angeles, California. Tel: (213) 628-2725. Email: jacco@anet.net. Internet: http://anet.net/apa/jaccc. Built in 1980 to preserve and encourage an appreciation of the Japanese heritage and cultural arts in the younger generations of Japanese Americans. Special annual events are geared to the family and the celebration of traditional cultural activities.

**Japanese American National Museum**, 369 East First Street, Los Angeles, CA 90012; (213) 625-0414. Weekly interactive children's day called Keiki/Parent day. Various festivals, arts and crafts classes, and a variety of other educational opportunities for children. Participates in annual Nisei Week festival in August, and the Little Tokyo Spring Festival in May. Also publishes a directory of Japanese American resources.

**Japanese Community Youth Council**, 2012 Pine Street, San Francisco, CA 94115; (415) 563-8052. Formed in 1970 to foster the educational, social, and cultural development of Japanese American Youth in San Francisco.

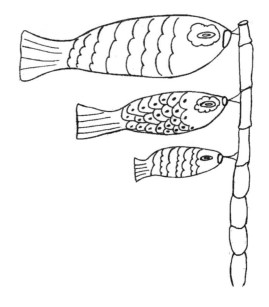

**Japanese Tea Garden**, Tea Garden Drive, Golden Gate Park, San Francisco; (415) 752-1171. Located next to the DeYoung and Asian Art Museum. Open daily 9 a.m.–6 p.m. (Mar–Sept) and 8:30 a.m.–6 p.m. (Oct–Feb). Admission is $1 for kids ages 6–12; $2 for adults.

**Los Angeles Children's Museum**, 369 East 1st Street, Los Angeles, CA 90099; (213) 625-0414. Often presents Japanese programs. Call in advance for dates and times.

**National Japanese American Historical Society**, 1855 Folsom Street, Suite 161, San Francisco, CA 94108; (415) 431-5007.

**Pacific Asia Museum**, 46 N. Los Robles Ave., Pasadena, CA 91101; (818) 449-2742. Collections include Japanese ceramics, textiles, and historic photographs. There are formally organized education programs for children and adults, a children's gallery, and a workshop. Open Wednesday to Sunday, 12 p.m. to 5 p.m. Admission is $1.50 for students; $3 non-members.

## Florida

**The Morikami Museum and Japanese Gardens**, 4000 Morikami Park Road, Delray Beach, FL 33446; (407) 495-0233. Museum, theater, library, classes, demonstrations, bonsai and Japanese gardens, a nature trail, and more. Summer TourPlus Program for children's groups combines a guided tour plus one or more hands-on activities or cultural presentations. Open daily 10 a.m.–5 p.m., except Mondays and major holidays. Admission is $1 for kids ages 6–18; $3.25 for adults.

## Hawaii

**Honolulu Academy of the Arts**, 900 South Beretania Street, Honolulu, HI 96814; (808) 532-8712. Weekly interactive children's day (Keiki/Parent Day); various children's festivals throughout the year. A branch of the Academy, the Linekona Art Center, offers art classes for children of all ages.

**Japanese Cultural Center of Hawaii**, 2454 South Beretania Street, Honolulu, HI 96826; (808) 945-7633. Special programs in conjunction with exhibits can be geared specifically for or include children as part of the audience. Includes art contests, children's games, entertainment, and more.

## Illinois

**Chicago Japanese American Historical Society**, 4954 N. Monticello, Chicago, IL 60625; (312) 267-6312. Creates programs and conducts research on the history of Japanese Americans in Chicago.

## Kentucky

**Greater Louisville Japanese Cultural Center**, Louisville, KY; (812) 941-2683.

## Massachusetts

**The Children's Museum**, Japan Program, 300 Congress Street, Boston, MA 02210-1034; (617) 426-6500. Open daily, 10 a.m.–5 p.m; Friday, 10 a.m.–9 p.m. Admission is $6 for kids; $7 for adults.

## New Jersey

**Seabrook Educational and Cultural Center,** Upper Deerfield Township Municipal Building, Highway 77, P.O. Box 5041, Seabrook, NJ 08302; (609) 451-1816. Presents the settlement and history of the many ethnic groups in New Jersey.

## New York

**Asian American Arts Centre,** 26 Bowery Street, 3rd Floor, New York, NY 10013; (212) 233-2154. The Centre offers pointed brush workshops and Asian dance and lectures in public schools, art classes and folk art instruction, and guided gallery tours. Open Tuesday to Friday, 12 p.m.–6 p.m.; Saturday, 3 p.m.–6 p.m. Admission is free.

**Museum of Migrating People,** Harry S. Truman High School, 750 Baychester Avenue, Bronx, NY 10475; (718) 904-5400. Collections include documents, artifacts, and memorabilia depicting the immigration experiences of Americans. Education programs are offered for children of all ages. Open school year, Monday to Friday, 9 a.m.–3 p.m. Closed school holidays. Admission is free.

**Statue of Liberty National Monument & Ellis Island,** Liberty Island, New York, NY 10004; (212) 363-7620. Exhibits on Ellis Island, American immigration, film; learning center & oral history program. Open daily Labor Day to Memorial Day, 9:15 a.m.–5 p.m.; Memorial Day to Labor Day, Monday to Friday, 9:15 a.m.–6 p.m., Saturday and Sunday, 9:15 a.m.–7 p.m. Admission is free.

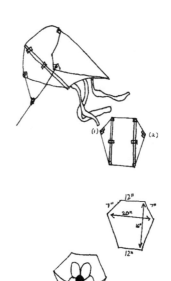

## Oregon

**The Western Treasure Valley Cultural Center,** P.O. Box 980, Ontario, OR 97914; (503) 889-8191. Scheduled to open in Spring, 1997, this museum will feature exhibits on Japanese American history, including a section on the 100th and 442nd Japanese Amreican military units that fought in World War II.

## Washington

**Japanese Heritage Historical Society,** 6927 Southeast Allen, Mercer Island, WA 98040; (206) 232-7487. Collects, preserves, and presents material about Japanese Americans in the Pacific Northwest.

The Wing Luke Asian Museum, 407 7th Avenue South, Seattle, WA 98104; (206) 623-5124. Permanent exhibit, "One Song, Many Voices: The Asian Pacific American Experience," covers the history of Japanese Americans in the Pacific NW together with the histories of other Asian Pacific Americans. Family programs one Saturday each month, and educational programs for children. Open Tuesday to Friday, 11 a.m.–4:30 p.m.; Saturday and Sunday, 12 p.m.–4 p.m. Admission is 75 cents for kids; $2.50 for adults. Free admission on Thursday.

## National

National Clearinghouse for U.S.-Japan Studies, 2805 East 10th Street, Suite 120, Bloomington, IN 47408-2698; (812) 855-3838. Email: japan@indiana.edu. World Wide Web: http://www.indiana.edu/~japan. Provides comprehensive information about educational resources on how to teach Japanese and Japanese American culture.

## ORGANIZATIONS

Buddhist Churches of America, National Headquarters, 1910 Octavia Street, San Francisco, CA 94109; (415) 776-5600. This is the central agency for Buddhism in the U.S.

United Methodist Board of Global Ministries, (800) 862-4246

## PUBLICATIONS

There are many interesting and informative fiction and nonfiction books about the Japanese American experience. A small selection of them has been provided here. Ask you local public librarian for more resources.

### Nonfiction
• Crost, Lyn. *Honor by Fire: Japanese Americans at War in Europe and the Pacific*, (1994).
• Hirabayashi, Lane Ryo. *Inside an American Concentration Camp*, (1995).
• Kawaguchi, Gary. *Tracing Our Japanese Roots*, (1995, John Muir Publications).
• Takaki, Ronald. *Issei and Nisei: The Settling of Japanese America*, (1995).
• Tsuchida, John Nobuya. *Reflections: Memoirs of Japanese American Women in Minnesota*, (1994).

### Fiction
• Brown, Janet Mitsui. *Thanksgiving at Obaachan's*, (1994). A Japanese American girl describes the Thanksgiving celebration at her grandmother's house.
• Coerr, Eleanor and Ed Young. *Sadako*, (1993). This is a story about a girl from Hiroshima who battles the atomic bomb disease, leukemia.
• Mochizuki, Ken. *Heroes*, (1995). Donnie, a Japanese American boy wants to play football after school, but his friends want to play war, with Donnie as the number one enemy.
• Say, Allen. *Grandfather's Journey*, (1993). The story of a young man's dilemma of loving two countries at the same time.

# INDEX